35 SIMPLE RULES FOR SUCCESS AND HAPPINESS: A GUIDE TO TRANSFORMING YOUR LIFE

UNLOCK JOY AND ACHIEVE YOUR BEST LIFE—ONE SIMPLE RULE AT A TIME

BY

TERRY BERNARD
YOUNG JR

Table of Contents

Rule #1:
Listen, Learn, Adapt

The Power of Listening, Learning, and Adapting

In an ever-changing world, one of the most valuable skills we can cultivate is the ability to listen, learn, and adapt. **Rule #1, "Listen, Learn, Adapt,"** encourages us to embrace a mindset of growth, curiosity, and flexibility, allowing us to thrive in any situation. This principle is about more than just hearing or adjusting; it's about intentionally tuning into the world around us, gaining wisdom from each experience, and evolving with resilience and openness.

This rule explores the importance of listening, learning, and adapting as a continuous cycle, offering insights into how these three actions can empower us to navigate life's complexities with confidence and grace. By mastering this cycle, we open ourselves to growth, resilience, and a deeper understanding of ourselves and others.

The Importance of Listening

Listening is essential for building stronger relationships, as active listening fosters trust, respect, and genuine connection, which creates deeper, more meaningful bonds. It also opens us to new perspectives, allowing us to understand viewpoints beyond our own experiences and assumptions. By listening attentively, we can enhance our problem-solving skills, gaining insights that help us see challenges from different angles and find better solutions. Additionally, listening improves our self-awareness as we become more reflective through feedback from others and our inner self. Finally, listening reduces misunderstandings and conflicts, creating an environment of clarity and mutual respect that strengthens communication and connection.

Listening is the foundation of empathy and understanding, making it a crucial step in learning and adapting effectively.

The Value of Learning

Learning is the process of absorbing and integrating new information, ideas, and perspectives, a lifelong pursuit that enriches our minds, expands our potential, and fosters growth in all areas of life. When we approach life as perpetual students, open to new knowledge and experiences, we cultivate resilience and curiosity. This openness enables us to make informed decisions, gain confidence, and pursue our goals with greater clarity. The value of learning is evident in the personal growth it brings, as each lesson, skill, or new perspective shapes us into more well-rounded individuals. Learning also increases adaptability; as we acquire a broader set of skills and knowledge, we become better equipped to handle change.

Additionally, learning strengthens problem-solving abilities by broadening our understanding and enabling us to approach challenges with creativity and insight. Knowledge also builds confidence, empowering us to make informed choices and tackle new challenges with assurance.

Furthermore, learning fosters a growth mindset, reinforcing the belief that we can continually improve and evolve and instilling a sense of possibility and resilience. Learning is a journey, not a destination. By staying open to growth, we cultivate the flexibility and resourcefulness needed to face life's challenges.

The Art of Adapting

Adapting is the ability to adjust to new circumstances, challenges, and opportunities with grace and resilience. It involves recognizing when change is necessary having the courage to pivot, letting go of rigid expectations, and embracing flexibility. This openness allows us to navigate life's uncertainties with confidence and positivity. Adapting doesn't mean compromising our values but finding new ways to honor them in various situations. The art of adapting includes resilience in the face of change, as adaptability strengthens our capacity to remain grounded even when life takes unexpected turns. It also increases our problem-solving flexibility, opening us to creative solutions and new paths forward when obstacles arise. Adaptability fosters openness to opportunities we might otherwise miss, enriching our lives with new experiences. Moreover, accepting and adapting to change reduces stress, teaching us to flow with circumstances instead of resisting them. Finally, each successful adaptation builds self-confidence, reinforcing our sense of agency and control as we handle whatever comes our way. Adapting is about growth, resilience, and the willingness to evolve. When we're open to change, we become stronger, more resourceful, and better equipped to thrive in any environment.

Practical Strategies for Listening, Learning, and Adapting

1. **Practice Active Listening**: When someone speaks, focus entirely on them without planning your response or letting your mind wander. Listen with empathy and ask questions to show your interest. This deep listening builds trust and opens doors to learning.

2. **Seek Out New Experiences**: Embrace opportunities to learn by stepping outside of your comfort zone. Try a new activity, travel, or take on a new challenge. Each new experience adds to your knowledge and builds your adaptability.

3. **Reflect on Your Experiences**: Take time to reflect on your experiences, successes, and challenges. Ask yourself what you learned, what you might do differently, and how you can apply those insights in the future. Reflection is a powerful tool for growth and adaptation.

4. **Stay Curious**: Cultivate a mindset of curiosity by asking questions, exploring new ideas, and seeking knowledge in everyday situations. Curiosity fuels learning and helps you approach life with an open, adaptable attitude.

5. **Embrace Change as an Opportunity**: Rather than fearing change, view it as a chance to learn and grow. Each change offers new lessons, and by choosing to adapt, you're strengthening your resilience and expanding your potential.

The Power of a Growth Mindset

A growth mindset—the belief that abilities and intelligence can be developed through effort and learning—is essential for mastering the cycle of listening, learning, and adapting. Those with a growth mindset view challenges as opportunities for development and see setbacks as temporary hurdles rather than permanent failures. This perspective fosters a willingness to embrace uncertainty with confidence and curiosity, enabling personal and professional growth. Cultivating a growth mindset involves embracing challenges as chances to learn, grow, and acquire new skills, recognizing that true growth often occurs outside of our comfort zones. It also means celebrating effort and progress rather than fixating solely on outcomes and understanding that each step, even if imperfect, contributes to long-term success.

Additionally, mistakes should be reframed as valuable learning experiences, prompting reflection and improvement for the future. Seeking feedback is another vital component, as constructive input from others provides insights that help refine skills and build resilience. Finally, cultivating patience and perseverance is key, acknowledging that growth takes time and that every small step forward is progress toward reaching your potential. A growth mindset empowers us to listen, learn, and adapt continuously, transforming each experience into an opportunity for self-discovery and growth.

4

<u>Real-life scenarios of Listening, Learning, and Adapting</u>

- **Career Changes**: Imagine you're transitioning to a new role at work with different responsibilities and challenges. By listening to feedback from colleagues, learning the skills required, and adapting to new expectations, you navigate the change with confidence, ultimately thriving in your new position.

- **Relationship Building**: In a relationship, whether personal or professional, listening is key to understanding each other's needs. By learning from your interactions and adapting your communication style, you build a stronger, more empathetic connection that fosters trust and understanding.

- **Personal Growth and Goal-Setting**: Suppose you're pursuing a fitness goal but find that your original plan isn't working as well as you'd hoped. By listening to your body, learning about alternative methods, and adapting your approach, you're able to make progress that aligns with your personal needs and goals.

- **Handling Unexpected Challenges**: Imagine a life event that disrupts your plans, such as a move or career change. By listening to your own feelings and those of the people around you, learning from the experience, and adapting to the new situation, you build resilience and navigate the challenge with confidence.

<u>Embracing Continuous Growth Through Listening, Learning, and Adapting</u>

The cycle of listening, learning, and adapting is a journey of continuous growth that enriches both our understanding of the world and our personal development. Each time we listen, we gain valuable insights that deepen our perspective. With every opportunity to learn, we expand our skills and broaden our horizons. As we adapt, we build resilience and carve out new pathways forward. This ongoing cycle forms the foundation of a dynamic and fulfilling life, one filled with opportunities for self-discovery and transformation. To live a life of continuous growth, it's essential to commit to lifelong learning by seeking new knowledge and opportunities for development in every situation. Staying open and flexible allows us to adjust our beliefs, actions, and mindset, enabling us to evolve with grace and resilience. Appreciating the process as a journey rather than a destination helps us value every lesson and experience as a step toward becoming the best version of ourselves. Nurturing a sense of curiosity keeps us engaged, encouraging us to approach each day with an eagerness to learn and a desire to understand more about ourselves and the world around us. Ultimately, Rule #1 is about embracing life with an open heart and an eager mind. By consistently listening, learning, and adapting, we not only transform our own lives but also contribute to a world where understanding, growth, and resilience thrive. This cycle becomes a powerful foundation for purpose, wisdom, and fulfillment, guiding us toward a life of continuous evolution.

Rule #2:
No Decision Based on Fear

The Freedom of Choosing Beyond Fear

Fear is a powerful emotion that often plays a role in our choices, whether we realize it or not. It can keep us from taking risks, pursuing our dreams, or making changes that could lead to growth and fulfillment. **Rule #2, "No Decision Based on Fear,"** encourages us to recognize and overcome fear as a driving force in our decisions, empowering us to make choices rooted in confidence, clarity, and genuine intention. When we stop letting fear dictate our actions, we open ourselves to a world of possibilities and discover the courage to pursue the life we truly desire.

This rule helps us understand how fear influences our decisions, ways to recognize fear-based thinking and practical strategies for choosing from a place of confidence and intention. By freeing ourselves from fear-based decisions, we build resilience, embrace our potential, and set the stage for a life of purpose and fulfillment.

Recognizing the Impact of Fear-Based Decisions

Fear-based decisions often stem from a desire to avoid discomfort, failure, or the unknown. While fear can serve as a protective instinct in certain situations, it's crucial to recognize when it begins to control our choices in ways that restrict growth and happiness. Allowing fear to dictate our decisions limits our options, keeps us playing it safe, and holds us back from experiences that could lead to fulfillment and self-discovery. This mindset can result in missed opportunities, as fear prevents us from seizing chances for positive change in our careers, relationships, or personal growth. It can also lead to stagnation, as we stay within our comfort zones and avoid challenges that might develop new skills or insights. Over time, fear-based choices often breed regret, leaving us with lingering "what ifs" as we wonder how life might have been different if we'd acted with courage. Moreover, constantly making decisions driven by fear reinforces anxiety and self-doubt, shifting our focus from potential success to a fixation on potential failure. Ultimately, these choices erode our authenticity, causing us to compromise our true desires and values and distancing us from the person we genuinely want to be. Recognizing and overcoming fear-based decision-making is essential to living a life of confidence, growth, and alignment with our truest selves. When we base decisions on fear, we are choosing limitation over possibility. Learning to recognize and overcome fear in our decision-making allows us to reclaim our power and make choices that align with our true selves.

Understanding the Root of Fear

To move beyond fear-based decisions, it's essential to understand where our fears come from. Fear is often rooted in past experiences, societal expectations, or self-doubt. By identifying these root causes, we can confront and address them, gaining the clarity and courage needed to make decisions from a place of confidence.

Common roots of fear include:

- **Fear of Failure**: Worrying about making mistakes or falling short can lead us to avoid risks or challenges that could lead to growth.

- **Fear of Rejection**: The desire for approval can make us hesitant to pursue paths that may be unconventional or unpopular, even if they align with our values and dreams.

- **Fear of the Unknown**: Uncertainty about the future often leads us to choose familiar, safe options rather than exploring new opportunities.

- **Fear of Judgement**: Concerns about how others will perceive us can cause us to conform to others' expectations rather than honoring our own desires.

- **Fear of Change**: The comfort of routine can make us resistant to change, even when it's necessary for our personal growth and well-being.

Understanding these fears allows us to examine them with compassion and curiosity, taking away some of their power. When we recognize that fear is a natural response, we can approach it with awareness and choose not to let it control us.

<u>Practical Strategies for Making Decisions Beyond Fear</u>

1. **Pause and Reflect**: When you notice fear influencing a decision, pause and reflect. Ask yourself if your choice is motivated by a desire to avoid discomfort or by a genuine alignment with your values. Taking a moment to step back creates space for clarity and perspective.

2. **Identify Your True Intentions**: Reflect on your true intentions behind each decision. Are you choosing out of fear or out of genuine desire? By focusing on your goals, values, and aspirations, you gain the clarity to make choices that align with your authentic self.

3. **Visualize the Outcome of Courage**: Imagine the outcome if you choose courage over fear. Visualizing success, fulfillment, or personal growth helps reinforce a positive outlook, making it easier to step beyond fear and take action.

4. **Practice Self-Compassion**: Fear often triggers self-doubt. Practice self-compassion by acknowledging your fears without judgment. Remind yourself that everyone experiences fear and that moving forward despite it is an act of strength.

5. **Focus on the Long-Term Impact**: Consider the long-term impact of each decision. Will choosing out of fear keep you stuck or lead to regret? By focusing on the bigger picture, you can make choices that support your growth and future well-being.

<u>Reframing Fear as a Tool for Growth</u>

While fear can feel limiting, it also plays a valuable role in personal growth. Instead of viewing fear as a barrier, we can see it as an indicator of areas where we have the potential to expand and evolve. Each time we confront fear, we strengthen our resilience, broaden our comfort zones, and build confidence. Fear can transform into a powerful tool for growth when we approach it with curiosity and a willingness to challenge ourselves. To reframe fear as a catalyst for growth, it's important to acknowledge fear as a natural part of the human experience. Recognizing it without judgment helps us understand that everyone faces fear, and it often signals opportunities for personal development. Fear can serve as a compass, pointing toward goals or decisions that might lead to meaningful growth and fulfillment. Embracing the discomfort that comes with facing fear allows us to push past limitations, reinforcing resilience and expanding our comfort zones with every step forward. Celebrating small victories along the way helps us recognize the courage it took to overcome fear, fueling our confidence to tackle future challenges. By reframing fear in this way, we shift our mindset from avoidance to opportunity, empowering ourselves to grow and thrive through each challenge we encounter.

<u>Real-Life Scenarios of Choosing Beyond Fear</u>

- **Career Decisions**: Suppose you're offered a new job opportunity, but it requires skills you're not fully confident in. Choosing beyond fear means embracing the role, knowing it offers a chance to grow. Rather than letting self-doubt dictate your decision, you focus on the opportunity for learning and development.

- **Pursuing a Passion**: Imagine you've always wanted to start a creative project but fear judgment or failure. Choosing beyond fear means taking the first step—signing up for a class, creating a portfolio, or sharing your work. Each small action builds confidence, helping you pursue your passion without being limited by fear.

- **Building New Relationships**: Meeting new people can be intimidating, especially if you fear rejection. Choosing beyond fear means opening yourself to new connections, engaging in conversation, and sharing who you are. By focusing on the potential for connection rather than the risk of rejection, you expand your network and build meaningful relationships.

- **Making a Major Life Change**: Suppose you're considering moving to a new city or starting a new career path, but fear holds you back. Choosing beyond fear means recognizing the potential for growth and fulfillment in the change rather than letting fear of the unknown keep you in place. Each bold choice brings you closer to a life aligned with your goals and values.

Building a Life Rooted in Confidence, Not Fear

By choosing not to make decisions based on fear, we create a life that reflects our true values, aspirations, and strengths. This mindset enables us to navigate challenges with resilience, approach opportunities with openness, and embrace change with confidence. When fear no longer holds the reins, we are free to pursue an authentic and fulfilling life grounded in purpose and self-belief. Living a life rooted in confidence rather than fear means trusting yourself by making decisions aligned with your values and goals, reinforcing your belief in your abilities and resilience with each choice. It also involves embracing uncertainty with curiosity viewing the unknown as an opportunity for exploration and growth. Taking purposeful action becomes central as you focus on creating what you desire instead of avoiding what you fear. Growth often requires stepping outside of your comfort zone, and by prioritizing growth over ease, you take courageous steps toward realizing your full potential. Each time you choose beyond fear, celebrate your courage; these moments build momentum, empowering you to continue making bold, confident choices. Ultimately, Rule #2 is about living boldly and authentically, with fear no longer dictating your path. By making decisions rooted in confidence, you unlock a life filled with possibilities, growth, and fulfillment, embracing the freedom to create the future you truly desire.

Rule#3:
Leave Things Better Than How You Found Them

The Power of Positive Impact

Rule #3 "Leave Things Better Than How You Found Them" is more than just a reminder to clean up after yourself; it's a call to make a meaningful and lasting impact on the world around you. Whether it's improving a space, uplifting a person, or contributing to a cause, this principle encourages us to approach life with care, responsibility, and a commitment to creating positive change. By leaving things better than how we found them, we enrich not only the world around us but also ourselves, cultivating a sense of purpose and fulfillment.

This rule explores the importance of this rule, its applications in various aspects of life, and practical ways to make it a guiding principle. When we strive to leave every interaction, environment, or situation better than it was before, we set a powerful example of responsibility, kindness, and growth.

Why This Rule Matters

The idea of leaving things better than how we found them is grounded in the belief that our actions create a ripple effect, influencing the world around us in meaningful ways. Every choice we make, no matter how small, has the power to either improve or diminish our surroundings. When we intentionally strive to create positive change, we not only enhance the immediate situation but also inspire others, strengthen communities, and contribute to a brighter future. This principle calls us to take ownership of our influence, using it to leave a lasting, positive legacy. It matters because it cultivates responsibility, fostering accountability and integrity as we take charge of our impact. It inspires growth by encouraging personal development and enhancing problem-solving skills. Acts of improvement also build connections, deepening trust and relationships with others. Moreover, leaving things better spreads positivity, creating a ripple effect that motivates others to follow suit, amplifying the collective impact. Finally, it aligns with purpose, reminding us that even small actions contribute to a greater good, giving our lives deeper meaning. By embracing this mindset, we transform everyday moments into opportunities for kindness, growth, and lasting improvement.

Applying This Rule in Everyday Life

Leaving things better than how we found them applies to every area of life, from physical spaces to relationships, professional settings, communities, and personal growth. By committing to improvement in these aspects, we cultivate a habit of mindfulness and contribution that shapes our actions and intentions. In physical spaces, whether it's a park, workplace, or home, leaving an area better demonstrates respect for others and the environment. This could involve cleaning up, organizing clutter, or enhancing the space with thoughtful additions like planting a tree or adding a creative touch. In relationships, every interaction is an opportunity to make someone feel valued, understood, and supported. Offering a listening ear, showing kindness, or providing encouragement strengthens bonds and fosters a positive emotional environment. Professionally, leaving things better can mean improving processes, mentoring a colleague, or contributing meaningfully to projects. Taking pride in these contributions leaves a lasting impression of care and professionalism. In communities, it might involve volunteering, supporting local initiatives, or simply being a responsible citizen. Acts like picking up litter, donating resources, or helping local businesses can create significant positive change. Lastly, this principle applies to personal growth by striving to improve yourself daily. Learning from experiences and nurturing your mind, body, and spirit ensures you leave your own self better than before. Together, these actions create a ripple effect of positivity and improvement in every sphere of life.

Practical Ways to Leave Things Better

1. **Take Ownership of Your Impact**: Acknowledge that your actions, big or small, contribute to the world around you. Whether it's a conversation, a task, or an environment, commit to making it better in some way.

2. **Start Small**: Improvement doesn't have to be monumental. Simple acts like tidying up, offering a compliment, or lending a helping hand can create meaningful change.

3. **Practice Active Listening**: In relationships, leaving things better often begins with understanding. Listen deeply to others, acknowledge their feelings, and respond with empathy.

4. **Be a Problem-Solver**: Look for opportunities to improve processes, systems, or spaces. Whether it's fixing something that's broken or suggesting a better way of doing things, small solutions add up.

5. **Lead by Example**: Inspire others by embodying this principle in your actions. When people see you consistently leaving things better, they're more likely to follow suit.

6. **Think Long-Term**: Consider the lasting impact of your actions. Choose sustainability, kindness, and improvement with the future in mind.

7. **Express Gratitude and Kindness**: Gratitude and kindness create a positive atmosphere and often encourage others to reciprocate, perpetuating the cycle of leaving things better.

The Ripple Effect of Positive Change

When we leave things better than how we found them, our actions don't just stop at the immediate impact—they create a ripple effect. A small improvement can inspire others to do the same, leading to collective progress and a stronger sense of community. For example, one person's decision to clean up a shared space can motivate others to keep it clean, while a kind gesture can inspire a chain reaction of kindness.

This ripple effect amplifies the power of our actions, demonstrating that even small efforts can lead to significant change. When we commit to making things better, we're not just improving one moment or place—we're contributing to a culture of care, responsibility, and growth.

Real-Life Scenarios of Leaving Things Better

- **In a Public Space**: Imagine walking through a park and noticing litter. Taking a moment to pick up a few pieces of trash not only improves the environment but also sets an example for others who may be inspired to do the same.

- **In a Conversation**: A friend shares their struggles with you. By actively listening, offering words of encouragement, and validating their feelings, you leave the interaction better by uplifting their spirit.

- **At Work**: Suppose you're working on a project and notice an inefficient process. Suggesting improvements or streamlining the workflow leaves the team in a better position for future success.

- **In Your Neighborhood**: Volunteering to help with community cleanup, starting a garden, or supporting local initiatives leaves a lasting impact that enhances the quality of life for everyone around you.

- **In Personal Development**: After experiencing a setback, you choose to learn from it and grow, leaving your mindset stronger and more resilient than it was before.

Living a Life of Positive Contribution

Rule #3 isn't just about isolated actions—it's about embracing a mindset of contribution and responsibility that influences every aspect of our lives. By committing to leaving things better than how we found them, we choose to live with intention, care, and purpose. This approach fosters personal growth, strengthens relationships, and creates a lasting legacy of positive impact. Living a life of positive contribution begins with being mindful of our actions, paying attention to how our choices affect others and the world around us, and striving to leave a positive mark wherever we go. It involves seeking opportunities for improvement, whether in our relationships, work, or community and recognizing that even the smallest acts of kindness and care contribute to the greater good. Taking pride in these small improvements reminds us that change often starts with simple actions.

Additionally, inspiring others to embrace this mindset amplifies its impact, creating a ripple effect of positivity and progress. Ultimately, Rule #3 is about crafting a life filled with meaning and purpose, where every interaction, environment, and relationship benefits from our presence. By leaving things better than we found them, we're not only improving the world around us but also building a legacy of kindness and positive change. Embrace this principle as a guiding light, and let your actions demonstrate the power of making the world a little better, one step at a time.

Rule #4:
Do Things Right, or Do Things Over

The Value of Doing Things Right

In a fast-paced world where shortcuts and quick fixes often take precedence, **Rule #4 "Do Things Right, or Do Things Over,"** reminds us of the importance of effort, precision, and quality. This principle isn't about perfectionism; it's about approaching our tasks, goals, and responsibilities with care, intention, and accountability. When we commit to doing things right the first time, we save time, energy, and resources while also cultivating a sense of pride in our work and integrity in our actions.

This rule explores why doing things right matters, the cost of cutting corners, and how to adopt a mindset of intentional effort. By living according to this rule, we enhance our personal and professional lives, build trust in our relationships, and foster growth and resilience.

Why Doing Things Right Matters

Doing things right the first time is about more than just efficiency; it reflects our character, values, and commitment to excellence. When we approach tasks thoughtfully and with diligence, we demonstrate respect for ourselves, others, and the work we undertake. This mindset not only yields better results but also instills confidence, trust, and a deep sense of accomplishment. By consistently delivering quality work, we build trust and credibility, as others see us as reliable and trustworthy, which strengthens both personal and professional relationships. Additionally, doing things right the first time saves time and effort by avoiding the need to redo tasks, preventing frustration and unnecessary repetition. This commitment to quality fosters personal growth, helping us develop discipline, attention to detail, and problem-solving skills that enhance both personal and professional development. Moreover, putting forth our best effort enhances pride in our work, providing fulfillment and a sense of achievement. Finally, quality work creates long-term success, standing the test of time in projects, relationships, and personal goals, as it lays a solid foundation for lasting accomplishments.

The Cost of Cutting Corners

When we rush through tasks or settle for "good enough," we often create more problems than we solve. While cutting corners may save time at the moment, it usually results in mistakes, frustration, and missed opportunities for growth. The cost of not doing things right can be significant, impacting both tangible resources and intangible outcomes such as trust, reputation, and self-confidence. The consequences of cutting corners are far-reaching: wasted time and resources from fixing mistakes or starting over; damaged relationships due to delivering subpar results that erode trust and credibility; missed opportunities for growth by avoiding the effort needed to build skills and discipline; increased stress and frustration from redoing work or addressing avoidable errors; and an erosion of self-worth as consistently cutting corners diminishes pride and a sense of accomplishment. Recognizing these costs highlights the value of committing to quality from the outset, fostering a mindset of intentional effort and care that leads to better results and personal fulfillment.

Practical Strategies for Doing Things Right

1. **Set Clear Goals and Expectations**: Before starting a task, take the time to define what success looks like. Clarity about your goals and standards ensures that you approach the task with focus and intention.

2. **Prioritize Preparation**: Proper planning and preparation are key to doing things right. Gather the necessary tools, information, and resources before you begin to minimize errors and inefficiencies.

3. **Break Tasks into Manageable Steps**: Large tasks can feel overwhelming, leading to rushed or incomplete work. Breaking them into smaller, actionable steps allows you to focus on each part, ensuring quality throughout.

4. **Adopt a Mindset of Excellence**: Approach every task with the mindset that your effort reflects your values. Strive for excellence, not perfection, aiming to deliver your best without undue pressure.

5. **Take Your Time**: Rushing often leads to mistakes. Allow yourself enough time to complete tasks thoroughly, ensuring attention to detail and reducing the need for rework.

6. **Seek Feedback and Reflect**: Feedback helps identify areas for improvement. Reflect on your work and seek input from others to refine your approach and deliver better results in the future.

7. **Learn from Mistakes**: If something does need to be redone, use it as a learning opportunity. Reflect on what went wrong, adjust your approach, and commit to doing it better next time.

<u>The Power of Redoing with Intention</u>

Sometimes, despite our best efforts, things don't go as planned. Rule #4 encourages us not to shy away from doing things over when necessary. Redoing something with intention and care presents an opportunity for growth, learning, and improvement. It's a chance to demonstrate resilience, refine our skills, and ultimately achieve a better outcome. Approaching rework with a positive mindset is key. Instead of viewing a redo as a failure, accept it as an opportunity to

20

make meaningful improvements and achieve greater success. Reflect on what didn't work, analyze the setbacks, and use those insights to refine your approach. Commit to the process as a way to develop discipline, enhance problem-solving skills, and gain a deeper understanding of your work. Redoing things with intention transforms what may seem like a setback into a stepping stone for progress, reinforcing the value of persistence and growth.

Real-Life Scenarios of Doing Things Right

- **At Work**: Imagine you're preparing a presentation for an important meeting. Rushing through it could result in unclear messaging or errors. Taking the time to research, plan, and rehearse ensures a polished, impactful presentation that reflects your professionalism.

- **In Relationships**: When resolving a conflict, approaching the conversation with care, empathy, and active listening ensures a stronger, more respectful outcome. Cutting corners by avoiding difficult topics or rushing the discussion can lead to unresolved issues.

- **In Personal Goals**: Suppose you're learning a new skill, like playing an instrument or building a fitness routine. Rushing through practice or skipping foundational steps may hinder your progress. Committing to consistent, quality effort helps you achieve meaningful, lasting results.

- **In Daily Responsibilities**: Tasks like cooking a meal, tidying your space, or writing an email may seem mundane, but doing them right demonstrates care and attention to detail, leaving you with a sense of pride and accomplishment.

Embracing a Mindset of Care and Quality

Rule #4 serves as a reminder to approach life with care, responsibility, and a commitment to quality. By doing things right or being willing to do them over, we cultivate resilience, integrity, and a sense of purpose. This mindset enriches both our personal and professional lives, strengthens relationships, and empowers us to pursue our goals with confidence. Embracing this rule begins with committing to quality, ensuring that every task, no matter how small, is approached with the intention of doing it well. It also involves taking responsibility for our work and outcomes and recognizing that our efforts reflect our values and character. Valuing growth is essential, as mistakes and setbacks provide opportunities to learn, improve, and grow stronger. Practicing patience is equally important, as understanding that quality requires time and effort and allowing ourselves the space to complete tasks thoroughly. By choosing to do things right or do them over, we align our actions with our values, fostering a life rooted in integrity, excellence, and continuous improvement. Rule #4 is more than a principle—it's a way of living that ensures our work, relationships, and achievements represent the best of who we are.

Rule #5:
Manage to the Option

The Power of Strategic Decision-Making

Life is full of choices, and each decision we make shapes our future in ways both big and small. **Rule #5 "Manage to the Option"** emphasizes the importance of creating, evaluating, and managing options to maximize opportunities and outcomes. It's about intentional decision-making, where you don't just react to circumstances but actively design paths forward. By managing to the option, you equip yourself with the tools to face challenges, seize opportunities, and align your actions with your long-term goals.

This rule explores the meaning of managing to the option, why it matters, and how to apply it effectively in your personal and professional life. When you approach life with this mindset, you're not just making decisions—you're creating a strategy for success.

What Does "Manage to the Option" Mean?

To manage to the option means prioritizing flexibility and foresight in decision-making. Rather than locking yourself into a single course of action, you actively consider alternatives, evaluate potential outcomes, and ensure you maintain the ability to pivot when necessary. This mindset combines thoughtful planning with adaptability, enabling you to respond effectively to change while staying aligned with your goals. Managing to the option involves creating choices by expanding your perspective and identifying multiple paths forward instead of defaulting to a single solution. It also requires evaluating outcomes by considering both the short-term and long-term implications of each option to achieve the best possible

23

results. Staying flexible is crucial, as it allows you to adjust your approach as circumstances evolve. Finally, this approach ensures that the options you pursue align with your values, priorities, and long-term vision for the future. By adopting this proactive and strategic mindset, you empower yourself to make more informed, intentional, and effective choices.

Why Managing to the Option Matters

Managing to the option is a vital skill because it equips you to navigate uncertainty with confidence and purpose. Life rarely goes exactly as planned, and the ability to adapt while remaining aligned with your goals is essential for long-term success. This mindset fosters intentional decision-making and minimizes the risk of feeling trapped in a single, limiting course of action. By maintaining flexibility, you build resilience, making it easier to handle unexpected challenges and setbacks. Exploring multiple options leads to better decision-making, as you're able to make more thoughtful and informed choices. Keeping your options open maximizes opportunities, allowing you to seize unexpected chances that align with your goals.

Additionally, careful evaluation reduces regrct, ensuring you're less likely to second-guess your decisions later. Knowing you've considered all possibilities enhances your confidence, empowering you to navigate complex situations with clarity and assurance. By managing to the option, you lay the groundwork for adaptability and purpose, enabling you to thrive in any circumstance.

Practical Steps to Manage to the Option

1. **Expand Your Perspective**: Before committing to a decision, brainstorm all possible options. Consider creative solutions and alternative approaches to ensure you're not overlooking potential paths.

2. **Weigh the Pros and Cons**: Evaluate the benefits and drawbacks of each option. Consider both short-term gains and long-term consequences to make a balanced choice.

3. **Stay Open to Change**: Recognize that circumstances can shift. Be prepared to revisit and adjust your options as new information or opportunities arise.

4. **Prioritize Alignment with Goals**: Focus on options that align with your core values and long-term objectives. A decision that fits your vision is more likely to lead to fulfillment and success.

5. **Plan for Flexibility**: Build flexibility into your decisions. For example, if you're committing to a new project or career path, identify ways to pivot or expand your approach if needed.

6. **Seek Input from Trusted Sources**: Consult with mentors, friends, or colleagues to gain diverse perspectives. Others may offer insights or ideas you hadn't considered.

7. **Take Action with Clarity**: Once you've evaluated your options, commit to a course of action with confidence. Even if adjustments are needed later, moving forward with clarity ensures progress.

<u>Managing to the Option in Different Areas of Life</u>

Managing to the option applies across various aspects of life, offering flexibility and foresight to navigate decisions effectively. In career decisions, this mindset involves exploring multiple paths when considering a change or advancement. Rather than focusing solely on a promotion, you might evaluate options like further education, a lateral move for skill-building, or entrepreneurship, ensuring your choice aligns with your professional goals while maximizing opportunities. In personal growth, managing to the option means trying different approaches to achieve development. If a particular fitness routine or learning strategy isn't working, you adapt and explore alternatives that better suit your needs and preferences. For relationships, this approach helps you navigate conflicts or transitions with empathy and intention. Instead of reacting impulsively, you thoughtfully consider ways to address challenges, fostering mutual respect and understanding. In financial planning, managing to the option might involve creating a budget that accommodates unexpected expenses or diversifying investments to minimize risk. This strategy helps you stay adaptable while working toward financial goals. Even in everyday challenges, such as a delayed morning commute, managing to the option ensures you're not locked into rigid plans. Having considered alternative routes or work-from-home options allows you to adjust seamlessly, demonstrating the value of this adaptable and strategic mindset in all areas of life.

The Role of Foresight and Flexibility

Managing to the option requires a balance of foresight and flexibility. Foresight allows you to anticipate potential challenges and opportunities, while flexibility ensures you can adapt to the unexpected. Together, these qualities enable you to remain proactive and intentional in your decision-making, transforming uncertainty into opportunity. Cultivating these skills involves practicing scenario planning, where you imagine different potential outcomes for a decision and prepare responses for each. Staying curious is also essential, as approaching decisions with curiosity and exploring "what if" scenarios can uncover new possibilities. Building resilience further strengthens your adaptability by encouraging you to view setbacks as opportunities to reassess and pivot. By combining foresight and flexibility, you're better equipped to navigate life's complexities with confidence and clarity, turning challenges into stepping stones for success.

- **Career Transition**: Suppose you're considering leaving your current job. Managing to the option means exploring different opportunities—whether it's switching industries, freelancing, or further education—before making a decision. This approach ensures your next step aligns with your long-term goals.

- **Relocating to a New City**: If you're planning a move, managing to the option involves researching multiple neighborhoods, job markets, and housing options. This way, you're prepared to adjust if your initial plans don't work out.

- **Planning an Event**: When organizing an event, managing to the option means having a backup plan for weather, vendors, or unexpected cancellations. By anticipating potential issues, you ensure the event's success regardless of circumstances.

- **Navigating Relationships**: In a relationship conflict, managing to the option means considering different ways to resolve the issue—open communication, seeking mediation, or taking time for reflection—before deciding on a course of action.

Living a Life of Strategic Possibility

Rule #5 is about more than just making decisions—it's about creating a life guided by intentional choices and abundant opportunities. By managing to the option, you empower yourself to navigate uncertainty, embrace change, and remain aligned with your goals. This mindset fosters resilience, creativity, and confidence, transforming challenges into stepping stones for growth. To live a life guided by this principle, stay proactive by anticipating challenges and opportunities and preparing with well-thought-out options. Remain adaptable, adjusting your course as circumstances evolve while keeping your long-term goals in focus. Embrace possibility by viewing decisions as opportunities to explore, grow, and shape the life you desire. Ultimately, managing to the option is about crafting a life rooted in flexibility, foresight, and purpose. By adopting this mindset, you ensure that each decision moves you closer to a future filled with possibility, fulfillment, and success.

Rule #6:
Do not live off past victories, do not relive past defeats

The Balance Between Reflection and Progress

Life is a journey forward, yet we often find ourselves tethered to the past, either relishing old victories or reliving past defeats. **Rule #6 "Do Not Live Off Past Victories, Do Not Relive Past Defeats"** reminds us that while reflection can provide valuable lessons, we must not allow ourselves to become stuck in what was at the expense of what could be. This rule encourages us to honor our past without being defined by it, maintaining a focus on growth, progress, and the opportunities ahead.

This rule explores how to find the balance between learning from the past and living in the present, why dwelling on either triumphs or failures can hinder growth, and practical strategies for letting go of what holds you back while embracing what moves you forward.

The Pitfalls of Living in the Past

When we cling too tightly to the past—whether through nostalgia for victories or regret over failures—we risk stagnation. Both extremes can prevent us from being fully present and proactive in shaping our future. Living off past victories may create a false sense of accomplishment, leading us to rest on our laurels instead of pursuing new challenges. On the other hand, reliving past defeats can trap us in a cycle of self-doubt and fear, undermining our confidence and willingness to take risks. While celebrating success is important, continuously dwelling on past triumphs can lead to complacency. You might find yourself thinking, *"I've already achieved enough,"* which can stifle ambition and curiosity. This mindset can create a plateau in personal and professional growth, leaving you unprepared for new challenges. Focusing on failures often amplifies feelings of regret and inadequacy. You might replay mistakes over and over, convincing yourself that they define your future. This can lead to fear of trying again or taking risks, ultimately holding you back from reaching your potential.

Embracing the Past as a Tool for Growth

The past is not meant to be a place where we live; it's a source of wisdom to guide us forward. Both victories and defeats hold valuable lessons, but their purpose is to inform, not to dictate. By adopting a growth-oriented mindset, we can reflect on the past constructively, using it as a springboard for improvement and progress. Victories remind us of what we're capable of and the rewards of effort and persistence. Reflecting on success can help identify the strategies, habits, and mindsets that contributed to those achievements. Use this knowledge to replicate and build upon those successes in new areas of life. Failures, while painful, are some of life's greatest teachers. They highlight areas for growth and offer insights into what didn't work. By analyzing setbacks without self-judgment, you can extract lessons that prepare you for future challenges, turning mistakes into stepping stones.

Practical Strategies for Moving Forward

1. **Celebrate and Let Go:** Acknowledge and celebrate your successes, but don't linger on them. Appreciate the moment, reflect on what you learned, and then channel that energy into pursuing new goals.

2. **Reframe Failures:** Instead of viewing failures as permanent setbacks, see them as opportunities for growth. Ask yourself, "What can I learn from this?" and use those lessons to improve your approach moving forward.

3. **Focus on the Present:** Practice mindfulness to stay grounded in the present moment. Whether you're setting goals or taking action, focus on what you can do today to create a better future.

4. **Set New Goals:** Continuously set goals that challenge and inspire you whether personal or professional, new objectives keep you focused on growth and prevent stagnation.

5. **Cultivate a Growth Mindset:** Embrace the belief that you can always improve and learn. This mindset encourages you to view both victories and defeats as part of a larger journey of progress.

6. **Avoid Comparison to Your Past Self:** While it's natural to compare yourself to who you were, focus on who you're becoming. Progress isn't about eclipsing past achievements but about consistent evolution.

The Power of Forward Momentum

Choosing not to live off past victories or relive past defeats creates a powerful sense of forward momentum. When we focus on the future, we open ourselves to possibilities that the past could never offer. Each day becomes an opportunity to redefine what success and growth look like, independent of prior experiences. Momentum comes from taking consistent, intentional actions toward your goals. Even small steps, when taken consistently, build energy and confidence, helping you move past the limitations of the past and into a future of limitless potential.

Real-Life Scenarios of Moving Beyond the Past

- **Career Advancement**: Imagine you've achieved a major milestone at work, such as a promotion or a successful project. While it's tempting to rest on that success, embracing Rule #6 means asking yourself, *"What's next?"* Focus on building new skills or tackling new challenges to continue growing in your career.

- **Overcoming Personal Setbacks**: Suppose you've faced a failure, such as a failed business venture or relationship. Rather than letting that defeat define you, analyze what went wrong, take the lessons learned, and approach the next opportunity with renewed determination and wisdom.

- **Creative Pursuits**: If you've experienced recognition for a creative achievement, such as publishing a book or completing an art piece, don't let that moment become the peak of your creativity. Challenge yourself to innovate and push boundaries, using past success as a foundation rather than a finish line.

- **Health and Wellness**: Perhaps you once achieved a fitness goal but have since fallen off track. Instead of lamenting lost progress, focus on creating a new plan that meets your current needs and circumstances, proving to yourself that growth is always possible.

<u>Living a Life of Continuous Growth</u>

Rule #6 encourages us to honor the past without being bound by it. By refusing to live off past victories or relive past defeats, we allow ourselves to fully embrace the present and create a future filled with new possibilities. This mindset fosters growth, resilience, and the belief that our best days are yet to come. To live by this rule, begin by acknowledging the past but avoiding the trap of dwelling there; reflect on your experiences to gather insights, then refocus on the present and future. Stay curious and ambitious by continuously seeking out new challenges, experiences, and opportunities for growth. Redefine success as progress, measuring it by your ability to move forward rather than clinging to what has already been achieved or lost. Ultimately, Rule #6 is a call to action that invites you to celebrate your accomplishments, learn from your setbacks, and use those experiences to build a life that is dynamic, purposeful, and always moving forward. By embracing this principle, you ensure that your greatest achievements and growth lie ahead, waiting to be discovered.

Rule #7:
If you can make them laugh, you can make them listen

The Transformative Power of Laughter

In a world filled with noise, capturing and holding someone's attention can be challenging. **Rule #7 "If You Can Make Them Laugh, You Can Make Them Listen"** reminds us that humor is a powerful tool for connection and communication. Laughter has the unique ability to break down barriers, foster understanding, and create an atmosphere where ideas can be shared more openly. By using humor effectively, we can engage others, make meaningful connections, and communicate with greater impact.

This rule explores the science and art of humor, why it fosters connection, and how to use it to enhance your ability to be heard and understood. When applied thoughtfully, humor becomes a bridge that transforms interactions, making your message resonate in ways that inspire and empower.

Why Humor Works

Humor has a disarming effect that puts people at ease, lightens the mood, and opens their minds to new ideas. Laughter triggers the release of endorphins, fostering trust and a sense of well-being. When people laugh, they feel more connected and receptive, making it easier to share perspectives and communicate effectively. Humor also makes complex or uncomfortable topics more approachable, allowing conversations to flow naturally. Its effectiveness in communication lies in several key benefits: it breaks down barriers by creating common ground and helping people feel more comfortable and engaged. A well-timed joke or witty comment captures attention, making listeners more focused and willing to engage. Humor also enhances retention, as messages delivered with humor are more memorable due to the positive emotions they evoke. It fosters trust by building camaraderie and encouraging open, honest communication. Additionally, humor diffuses tension, easing conflict or awkwardness and creating a safe space for meaningful dialogue. These qualities make humor a powerful tool for connecting with others and delivering impactful messages.

The Balance Between Humor and Message

While humor is a powerful tool, it must be used thoughtfully to ensure it supports rather than detracts from your message. The goal is to enhance communication, not overshadow it. Humor should feel natural and align with the context of the conversation or audience, as misused humor can backfire, alienating listeners or undermining your credibility. To strike the right balance, it's essential to know your audience and tailor your humor to their preferences, sensitivities, and the context in which you're communicating. Keep your humor relevant to the topic or message, ensuring it adds value rather than derailing the conversation. Avoid insensitivity by steering clear of jokes that might offend or marginalize others, as this can erode trust and connection. Most importantly, be authentic—use humor that aligns with your personality and communication style to keep it genuine and relatable. When humor is applied appropriately and authentically, it becomes a powerful tool to connect, communicate, and inspire effectively.

How to Use Humor to Make People Listen

1. **Start with a Lighthearted Opener**: Begin a conversation, presentation, or meeting with a relatable or funny anecdote. This sets a positive tone and encourages engagement.

2. **Use Humor to Illustrate Points**: Analogies, jokes, or playful comparisons can make complex ideas easier to understand and remember. Humor simplifies without trivializing.

3. **Be Self-Deprecating**: Lighthearted jokes at your own expense show humility and make you more relatable. Just ensure it doesn't undermine your authority or message.

4. **Read the Room**: Pay attention to how your humor is received. Adjust your approach based on the audience's reactions to maintain connection and respect.

5. **Incorporate Playful Wordplay**: Clever language or puns can add levity to conversations, making your message more engaging and memorable.

6. **End on a Positive Note**: Wrap up with a humorous remark or uplifting comment to leave a lasting, positive impression.

The Science Behind Laughter and Connection

Laughter is not just an emotional response; it's a physiological and psychological phenomenon. When we laugh, our bodies release endorphins, reducing stress and fostering feelings of happiness. This creates a sense of connection and trust, which are critical for effective communication. Studies have shown that shared laughter strengthens social bonds, making people more likely to listen and collaborate.

Humor also activates the brain's reward system, making the listener more engaged and attentive. A well-placed joke can spark curiosity and interest, ensuring your message lands more effectively.

- **Professional Presentations:** A speaker begins a presentation on workplace efficiency with, *"Why don't we ever have time to do it right, but always find time to do it over?"* The humor resonates with the audience's shared experience, opening the door for a deeper discussion about effective practices.

- Resolving Conflict: During a heated team discussion, someone interjects with a lighthearted remark, like, "Okay, folks, we're not curing cancer here—let's take a breath." The humor diffuses tension, allowing the group to refocus on problem-solving.

- **Teaching or Mentoring:** A teacher struggling to engage students uses humor, saying, *"If procrastination were an Olympic sport, this class would be gold medalists!"* The laughter breaks the ice, encouraging students to participate.

- **Personal Relationships:** A friend dealing with a difficult situation is cheered up by a playful comment, like, *"Well, if life gives you lemons, at least we have margarita mix!"* The humor provides a moment of levity, creating space for deeper conversation.

Developing Your Humor Skills

If humor doesn't come naturally, don't worry—it's a skill that can be developed with practice and awareness. To cultivate your sense of humor, start by observing comedians or skilled speakers to see how they use humor to engage and connect with their audience. Experiment in low-stakes settings by practicing humor in casual conversations to discover your natural style. Reflect on your personal experiences and share lighthearted stories or lessons from your life to create relatable and genuine humor. Learn to laugh at yourself by embracing imperfections and approaching life with a playful mindset, which makes humor feel more effortless and authentic. The key is to remain true to yourself and adaptable, letting your humor naturally enhance your communication and connection with others.

Living by Rule #7

Rule #7 is more than a strategy for effective communication—it's a reminder of the power of joy and connection in our interactions. Laughter bridges the divide, fosters understanding, and creates an environment where people are not just willing to listen but eager to engage. Living by this rule involves approaching life lightly, finding humor in everyday moments to connect with others, and diffusing tension. It means communicating with joy and using laughter as a tool to build trust and understanding in your conversations. At the same time, it's essential to balance humor with purpose, ensuring it enhances your message rather than distracting from it. Ultimately, Rule #7 invites you to embrace humor as a way to open doors, strengthen relationships, and make your voice heard. If you can make them laugh, you can make them listen—and when they listen, your message has the potential to create a lasting impact.

Rule #8:
Fall Seven Times. Stand Up Eight

Life is full of challenges, setbacks, and unexpected twists. At times, the weight of adversity may feel insurmountable, but it is in these moments that our true strength emerges. **Rule #8 "Fall Seven Times, Stand Up Eight"** draws inspiration from the timeless Japanese proverb that speaks to the heart of resilience. It reminds us that what defines us is not how many times we fall but how many times we rise, learn, and grow stronger. Each fall is not an end but a step in the journey toward becoming our best selves.

This rule explores the transformative power of resilience, the lessons hidden within failures, and how to cultivate the inner strength to keep standing no matter how many times life knocks you down. By embracing this mindset, you can turn every setback into an opportunity for growth and triumph.

Resilience: The Power to Rise Again

Resilience is the ability to recover, adapt, and persevere in the face of adversity. It's not about avoiding challenges but about finding the strength to confront them and emerge stronger. Each time we fall, we are presented with a choice: to stay down or to rise and try again. Choosing to rise builds resilience, fostering a mindset that transforms obstacles into stepping stones.

The essence of "Fall Seven Times, Stand Up Eight" lies in the understanding that failure is not final. Instead, it is part of the process of growth and self-discovery. With each fall, we learn more about our capabilities, refine our strategies, and strengthen our determination. Resilience is the force that keeps us moving forward, helping us navigate life's challenges with courage and perseverance.

Learning Through Failure

Failure is often misunderstood as something to be feared or avoided, yet it is one of life's greatest teachers, offering invaluable lessons that guide us toward greater wisdom and success. Each setback provides clarity and insight, highlighting what doesn't work and pointing us toward better solutions. It tests our resolve, building resilience and strength to face future challenges. Failures also foster humility and self-awareness, encouraging us to accept our imperfections and embrace the learning process. Moreover, setbacks push us to think creatively and adapt to new circumstances, sparking innovation and growth. When we shift our perspective to view failure as an opportunity rather than a defeat, we unlock the potential to achieve more than we ever thought possible. By embracing these lessons, failure transforms from a source of pain into a powerful catalyst for personal evolution.

The Courage to Keep Standing

Standing up after a fall requires courage and a belief in your ability to overcome. It's not about denying the pain or difficulty but about choosing to move forward despite it. This courage is fueled by hope, determination, and an unwavering belief in the possibility of a better future.

Practical Steps to Cultivate Resilience:

1. **Accept the Fall**: Acknowledge the setback without judgment or denial. Acceptance is the first step toward recovery and growth.

2. **Reflect and Learn**: Analyze what led to the fall. What lessons can you take away? Use this insight to adjust your approach moving forward.

3. **Reframe the Narrative**: Instead of seeing the fall as a failure, view it as a necessary step in your journey. Every setback is a chance to grow stronger.

4. **Set Small Goals**: Focus on incremental progress. Small, achievable steps rebuild confidence and momentum after a setback.

5. **Build a Support System**: Surround yourself with people who uplift and encourage you. A strong network provides strength and perspective in difficult times.

6. **Practice Self-Compassion**: Treat yourself with kindness and patience. Resilience grows when you permit yourself to be imperfect.

The Ripple Effect of Resilience

Resilience doesn't just impact our ability to overcome challenges—it inspires those around us. When we rise after a fall, we demonstrate strength, hope, and the power of perseverance. This ripple effect encourages others to face their own challenges with courage and determination, creating a cycle of growth and inspiration.

Real-Life Applications of Resilience

- **Career Challenges:** A professional setback, such as a failed project or job loss, can feel devastating. By embracing Rule #8, you acknowledge the disappointment, learn from the experience, and refocus on new opportunities. Each step forward builds resilience and prepares you for future success.

- **Personal Growth:** Suppose you've faced a personal failure, like not achieving a goal you worked hard for. Standing up again means reassessing your approach, seeking guidance, and using the experience as fuel to push toward your aspirations.

- **Relationships:** In relationships, misunderstandings and conflicts are inevitable. Resilience means learning from mistakes, communicating with empathy, and choosing to rebuild trust and connection.

- **Health and Wellness:** A health setback, like an injury or lapse in fitness goals, can feel discouraging. Standing up again involves setting realistic goals, staying committed to recovery, and celebrating progress along the way.

<u>Living by Rule #8</u>

To live by Rule #8 is to approach life with a mindset of persistence and possibility, accepting that falls are inevitable but choosing to rise each time with renewed strength and determination. This perspective not only equips you to navigate challenges but also empowers you to embrace life fully, seeing every setback as an opportunity for growth. Embodying Rule #8 means embracing imperfection and recognizing that failure is an essential part of the journey toward success. It involves celebrating each comeback taking pride in your resilience and progress with every step forward. Staying future-focused helps you keep your eyes on your goals, using challenges as motivation to continue striving. "Fall Seven Times, Stand Up Eight" is more than a proverb—it's a way of life, a call to embrace resilience, learn from failure, and keep moving forward no matter how many times you stumble. By living this principle, you build the strength to face life's challenges and the courage to pursue your dreams. Each time you rise, you reaffirm your ability to grow, adapt, and thrive, proving that the power to overcome lies within you.

Rule #9:
Always fight battles on your own terms

The Art of Choosing Your Ground

Life is full of challenges, some imposed upon us and others chosen willingly. **Rule #9, "Always Fight Battles on Your Own Terms"** emphasizes the importance of self-determination and strategic action in the face of conflict or adversity. It's about knowing your strengths, understanding the landscape, and choosing how and when to engage to maximize your chances of success. By fighting battles on your own terms, you maintain control, preserve your energy, and align your actions with your values and goals.

This rule delves into the essence of the deterministic experience, exploring the importance of self-awareness, strategic thinking, and deliberate action. It offers practical strategies to navigate life's challenges with confidence and purpose, ensuring you're not just reacting to circumstances but actively shaping outcomes in your favor.

Why Fighting on Your Own Terms Matters

Fighting on your own terms is about reclaiming agency and refusing to let others dictate the rules of engagement. Allowing external forces to set the conditions risks pulling you into situations where you are disadvantaged, overwhelmed, or diverted from your priorities. By setting your own terms, you align your actions with your strengths, values, and objectives, positioning yourself for success. This approach offers several key benefits: maintaining control by dictating when and how you engage, avoiding impulsive reactions or emotional decision-making, playing to your strengths by leveraging your unique skills, knowledge, and resources to increase your chances of success; preserving energy by engaging strategically and avoiding unnecessary conflicts; minimizing risks by carefully choosing battles that matter and avoiding unnecessary harm or failure; and aligning your actions with your long-term goals rather than serving someone else's agenda. Adopting this mindset shifts the balance of power, enabling you to face challenges with intention, clarity, and focus.

The Role of Self-Awareness in Choosing Battles

Before you can fight on your own terms, you must first understand yourself. Self-awareness is the foundation of strategic decision-making, allowing you to recognize your strengths, weaknesses, values, and priorities. Without this clarity, you risk engaging in battles that drain your energy and derail your progress. To cultivate self-awareness, ask yourself key questions: What are my strengths and resources? Identify the skills, knowledge, and assets you bring to the table. What are my values? Clarify what matters most to you to ensure your actions align with your principles. What are my goals? Understand your long-term aspirations to prioritize battles that move you closer to achieving them. What are my limits? Acknowledge your boundaries to avoid overextending yourself or engaging in unwinnable conflicts. By developing this level of self-awareness, you gain the clarity and focus to choose battles that align with your strengths and priorities, positioning yourself for meaningful success.

Practical Strategies for Fighting on Your Own Terms

1. **Choose Your Battles Wisely:** Not every fight is worth your time or energy. Focus on conflicts that matter, align with your goals, and offer a clear path to resolution.

2. **Set the Conditions for Engagement:** Take control of when, where, and how you address challenges. This ensures you are prepared and positioned to succeed.

3. **Leverage Your Strengths:** Use your unique skills, knowledge, and resources to your advantage. Avoid fighting on terms that exploit your weaknesses.

4. **Stay Emotionally Grounded:** Emotional reactions can cloud judgment and lead to impulsive decisions. Practice mindfulness and respond with intention rather than reacting out of anger or fear.

5. **Know When to Walk Away:** Sometimes, the best strategy is not to engage. If a battle doesn't serve your goals or values, walking away can be a powerful act of self-preservation.

6. **Be Strategic, Not Reactive:** Plan your actions with foresight and deliberation. Avoid being drawn into conflicts by others' urgency or provocation.

The Importance of Patience and Perspective

Fighting battles on your own terms requires patience and perspective, as it often means resisting the pressure to act hastily or respond emotionally. By taking the time to prepare and thoughtfully assess the situation, you position yourself for success while maintaining control of your narrative. Cultivating patience and perspective involves pausing before acting to give yourself space to think critically before engaging in any conflict. It also means focusing on the big picture by asking how the battle aligns with your long-term goals and whether it's worth pursuing. Practicing emotional regulation through techniques like deep breathing or journaling helps you process emotions and approach decisions with a clear mind. With patience and perspective, you can tackle challenges with clarity and confidence, ensuring you engage only when it aligns with your best interests and objectives.

<u>Real-Life Applications of Fighting on Your Own Terms</u>

- **Workplace Challenges:** Imagine you're facing criticism or opposition at work. Instead of reacting impulsively, take the time to gather evidence, identify allies, and address the issue in a setting where you feel confident and supported. By controlling the terms of the conversation, you're more likely to achieve a positive outcome.

- **Personal Relationships:** In a disagreement with a loved one, emotions can run high. Fighting on your terms means pausing to reflect on your feelings and needs before addressing the issue calmly and constructively. This approach fosters understanding and resolution rather than escalation.

- **Financial Decisions:** When dealing with financial negotiations, such as buying a car or negotiating a salary, fighting on your terms involves doing thorough research, setting clear boundaries, and negotiating from a position of knowledge and confidence.

- **Health and Wellness:** If you're addressing a health challenge, fighting on your terms means seeking second opinions, choosing treatments that align with your values, and advocating for your needs to ensure the best possible outcome.

<u>Living by Rule #9</u>

To live by Rule #9 is to embrace self-mastery and strategic thinking in every aspect of life. It involves understanding your strengths, setting clear boundaries, and choosing to engage only in battles that align with your goals and values. This approach empowers you to act with intention, conserve your energy, and focus on achieving meaningful outcomes. Key principles of living by Rule #9 include self-awareness, which means knowing your strengths, values, and goals to make informed decisions; intentionality, which encourages engaging only in battles that truly matter and support your purpose; strategic action, which involves planning your approach to maximize the likelihood of success; and emotional resilience, which helps you stay grounded and focused even in the face of adversity. By adopting this mindset, you reclaim control over your life, ensuring that every challenge becomes an opportunity to grow, succeed, and thrive on your own terms. Rule #9 is not just about winning battles—it's about living with purpose, clarity, and power.

Rule #10:

Be strong in the face of strength and humble with those who are weak. (The Compassion Rule)

In a world that often values power and dominance, **Rule #10, "Be strong in the face of strength and humble with those who are weak,"** offers a balanced approach to navigating relationships, challenges, and personal growth. This rule reminds us that true strength is not about overpowering others but about standing firm when faced with opposition while extending kindness and humility to those who need support. It's a call to lead with both resilience and compassion, embracing a duality that defines character and builds meaningful connections.

This rule explores how to embody strength without arrogance and humility without weakness, providing practical strategies to live a life guided by both courage and compassion.

The Dual Nature of Strength

Strength is often associated with power, confidence, and assertiveness, but true strength also requires restraint, empathy, and wisdom. Being strong in the face of strength means standing firm in your values and beliefs when challenged demonstrating confidence without aggression. On the other hand, being humble with those who are weak involves recognizing their vulnerability and offering support without condescension. This balance of strength and humility fosters respect, trust, and genuine connection in all areas of life. Strength without arrogance matters because it earns respect rather than fear, builds resilience under pressure by reinforcing your values, and inspires others through leadership rooted in integrity. Similarly, humility with the vulnerable is essential for building trust, as genuine humility deepens relationships and empowers others by offering kindness and understanding that uplifts and encourages growth. It also cultivates empathy, allowing us to see the humanity in others and fostering meaningful connections through compassion.

The Art of Being Strong in the Face of Strength

Standing firm in the face of strength means holding your ground without resorting to intimidation or hostility. It's about demonstrating confidence in your abilities and values, even when challenged by those with power or authority.

Practical Strategies for Being Strong:

1. **Know Your Worth**: Cultivate self-awareness and confidence in your abilities. When you know your value, external pressure becomes less intimidating.

2. **Communicate Assertively**: Use clear, respectful communication to stand your ground. Assertiveness conveys confidence without aggression.

3. **Maintain Emotional Control**: Stay calm under pressure. Emotional resilience helps you respond thoughtfully rather than react impulsively.

4. **Stay True to Your Values**: Align your actions with your principles, even in challenging situations. Integrity is a hallmark of true strength.

The Art of Being Humble with Those Who Are Weak

Humility with those who are weak is about recognizing vulnerability and offering support with kindness and respect. It's about lifting others without diminishing their dignity, empowering them to find their own strength.

Practical Strategies for Being Humble:

1. **Listen Actively**: Give your full attention to those in need. Active listening validates their feelings and builds trust.

2. **Offer Support Without Overstepping**: Help others in a way that empowers rather than patronizes. Focus on enabling their independence and growth.

3. **Practice Gratitude**: Recognize your own privileges and blessings. Gratitude fosters empathy and humility.

4. **Lead by Example**: Show compassion and humility in your actions, inspiring others to do the same.

Balancing Strength and Humility in Everyday Life

Balancing strength and humility requires mindfulness and intention. It's about knowing when to stand firm and when to step back, recognizing that both approaches are essential for meaningful relationships and personal growth.

Examples of Balancing Strength and Humility:

- **In the Workplace**: When negotiating with a confident counterpart, hold your ground with professionalism and clarity. When mentoring a junior colleague, approach with patience and encouragement.

- **In Relationships**: During a disagreement with a partner, assert your feelings respectfully. When your partner is struggling, offer empathy and support without judgment.

- **In Leadership**: Lead your team with decisiveness and confidence during challenges. Celebrate their contributions with humility and gratitude.

Living by Rule #10

To live by Rule #10 is to embrace the duality of strength and humility, recognizing that both are essential for personal and interpersonal harmony. Being strong in the face of strength allows you to demonstrate confidence, resilience, and integrity, standing firm in your values without succumbing to aggression. Meanwhile, being humble with those who are weak embodies compassion, kindness, and humanity, uplifting others with care and respect. Living by this principle means balancing power with grace, using your strength to uphold your values rather than dominate others. It involves empowering rather than overpowering, extending kindness and humility to support and foster the growth of those in need. Finally, it calls for leading with compassion, blending resilience with empathy to inspire trust and build meaningful connections. By combining strength and humility, you create a life rooted in respect, purpose, and authentic relationships.

Rule #10 is a reminder that true strength is not about overpowering others, and true humility is not about diminishing yourself. It's about finding the balance that allows you to stand firm in your convictions while lifting others with compassion. By living this principle, you cultivate respect, trust, and meaningful connections, creating a life rooted in integrity and empathy. In embracing strength and humility, you embody the best of both worlds, proving that leadership is not about dominance but about the courage to uplift and inspire.

Rule #11:
Do Not Loan What You Can't Lose

The Principle of Sustainable Generosity

Rule #11 "Do Not Loan What You Can't Lose" is more than financial advice; it's a philosophy that applies to relationships, time, energy, and emotional investment. It's a reminder to practice generosity responsibly, ensuring that the help we extend to others doesn't jeopardize our own well-being. This rule encourages us to give thoughtfully, balancing compassion with self-preservation and setting boundaries that allow us to be both kind and sustainable in our support. It is important to explore the deeper meaning behind Rule #11, why it's essential for maintaining balance in life, and practical strategies for applying this principle in financial and emotional contexts.

The Cost of Overextending

Generosity is a beautiful quality, but when it comes at the expense of our own stability, it can lead to stress, resentment, and even burnout. Overextending—whether financially, emotionally, or with your time—often creates more problems than it solves, leaving both you and the recipient in a precarious situation. When we loan beyond what we can afford to lose, we place ourselves at risk of financial strain, emotional exhaustion, or strained relationships. This rule is not about withholding generosity but about ensuring that our giving is sustainable and aligned with our own well-being.

Financial Application: Loaning Money Thoughtfully

In financial matters, loaning money can be a source of tension, especially when expectations and boundaries are unclear. Rule #11 encourages us to consider the impact of lending before we act, ensuring that we're not compromising our own financial stability.

Guidelines for Financial Generosity:

1. **Treat Loans as Gifts**: When loaning money, consider the possibility that it may not be repaid. If you can't afford to lose the amount, reconsider the loan.

2. **Set Clear Expectations**: If you choose to lend, discuss repayment terms and timelines upfront to avoid misunderstandings.

3. **Prioritize Your Stability**: Ensure your own financial needs—such as savings, bills, and future goals—are secure before offering assistance.

Emotional and Time Investment

This principle goes beyond financial generosity to include the emotional and time investments we make in others. Whether it's offering emotional support, mentoring, or assisting with a project, it's crucial to evaluate whether you can give without compromising your own well-being. To manage these investments responsibly, start by knowing your limits—be honest about your emotional bandwidth and the time you can realistically dedicate before committing to help. Give without expectation, offering your support because you genuinely want to, not because you anticipate something in return. Most importantly, protect your energy by recognizing when your efforts begin to drain your own resources and set boundaries to preserve your well-being. By doing so, you ensure that your support remains sustainable and meaningful.

The Importance of Boundaries

At the heart of Rule #11 is the concept of boundaries, which ensure that generosity doesn't lead to self-sacrifice or resentment. Healthy boundaries allow you to give freely while protecting your own needs and well-being. To set effective boundaries, start by communicating clearly—be upfront about what you can and cannot offer. Understand that it's okay to say no when giving would stretch you too thin, and recognize that declining is an act of self-preservation, not selfishness. If you're unable to meet a request, offer alternatives, such as providing advice or referrals, to show support in a way that aligns with your capacity. By setting boundaries, you create a balance that makes your generosity sustainable and meaningful.

Real-Life Applications of Rule #11

- **Loaning Money:** A friend asks to borrow a significant amount of money. Before agreeing, assess whether losing that money would create financial hardship for you if it would, offer a smaller amount as a gift instead, avoiding potential strain on your finances and relationship.

- **Offering Emotional Support:** A colleague frequently vents about their problems, consuming hours of your time. While you want to be supportive, recognize when it's impacting your own mental health. Set limits, such as scheduling specific times to talk or suggesting professional help.

- **Volunteering Time:** A community project requests your involvement, but you're already overcommitted. Instead of stretching yourself further, decline politely and recommend someone else who might be able to contribute.

The Balance Between Generosity and Self-Preservation

Living by Rule #11 doesn't mean being selfish—it means practicing mindful generosity. It's about giving what you can without depleting yourself, ensuring that your support remains sustainable and meaningful. This balance allows you to be a source of help and kindness while maintaining your own stability and peace of mind.

Living by Rule #11

To live by Rule #11 is to embrace responsible generosity, recognizing that true giving stems from a foundation of strength and balance. By understanding your limits and setting clear boundaries, you can offer support that uplifts others without compromising your own well-being. This principle involves giving thoughtfully by assessing your capacity before offering help, setting boundaries to preserve your resources, and prioritizing sustainability to ensure your stability before assisting others. Ultimately, Rule #11 empowers you to give from a place of abundance rather than scarcity, fostering relationships and acts of generosity that are both meaningful and enduring. It serves as a reminder that the best way to help others is by ensuring you remain strong, secure, and capable of providing support.

Rule #12:
Finish what you start

The Power of Completion

Starting something new often feels invigorating, fueled by the thrill of possibility and the spark of inspiration. But as time goes on, the enthusiasm can wane, and the finish line can feel increasingly out of reach. **Rule #12 "Finish What You Start"** is about overcoming this natural dip in motivation, embracing discipline, and committing to seeing things through to completion.

Whether it's a project, a commitment, or a personal goal, finishing what we start is a practice of resilience, integrity, and self-respect. This rule will explore why following through matters, how to overcome the inevitable obstacles along the way and practical strategies for nurturing the habit of completion.

Why Finishing Matters

When we finish what we start, we cultivate a sense of accomplishment, building trust in ourselves and showing others that we're reliable and capable. Completion is more than just ticking an item off a checklist—it's a declaration of perseverance, proof that we're willing to put in the work, and a testament to our resilience. Each time we leave something unfinished, we reinforce the habit of stopping short and diminishing our own sense of reliability. Finishing, on the other hand, builds momentum, reinforcing our confidence and self-efficacy. This momentum empowers us to tackle bigger challenges and dream bolder dreams, knowing we have what it takes to bring them to life.

The Common Roadblocks to Completion

Everyone encounters obstacles on the path to finishing, whether it's boredom, self-doubt, or fear of failure. Recognizing these roadblocks is the first step to overcoming them. One common challenge is the excitement dip, where the initial enthusiasm fades, and the task starts to feel like a chore—a temporary but normal phase. Perfectionism can also hinder progress, as the drive to make something flawless keeps us stuck in endless tweaks, afraid to declare it "finished." Fear of failure—or even success—can be another barrier, as completing a task means putting it out into the world to be judged, often leading to procrastination or avoidance. Finally, overwhelm can strike when a project feels so big that we don't know where or how to start. By understanding these challenges, we can develop strategies to tackle them effectively, ensuring we reach the finish line no matter how distant it seems.

Practical Strategies for Finishing What You Start

1. **Break It Down into Manageable Steps:** When a project feels overwhelming, break it into smaller, achievable steps. Define clear, actionable milestones, and focus on completing each step one at a time. As you accomplish each mini-goal, you'll build momentum toward the finish line.

2. **Commit to a Schedule:** Set aside dedicated time to work on your project each day or week, and stick to it. Treat this time as a non-negotiable appointment, just like a meeting or an important commitment. Consistency builds habits, and habits make it easier to finish.

3. **Set a Completion Deadline:** Deadlines provide accountability and a sense of urgency. Create realistic but challenging deadlines for each stage of your project. Share these deadlines with someone who can check in on your progress—accountability can be a powerful motivator to see things through.

4. **Visualize the Finish Line:** Take a moment to imagine the satisfaction of finishing your project. Visualize the pride and sense of achievement you'll feel, and let this vision motivate you. Keep this visualization in mind whenever motivation wanes as a reminder of why finishing is worth it.

5. **Push Through the Dip:** When enthusiasm dips, remind yourself that this feeling is temporary. Push through by focusing on the task at hand rather than the finish line. Sometimes, taking a small step forward—no matter how uninspired—will reignite your drive to complete the journey.

Embracing Discipline Over Motivation

Finishing what you start requires discipline more than fleeting motivation. Motivation is unpredictable and can fade quickly, but discipline is grounded in habits and resilience. Discipline is the commitment to continue when the excitement fades, the decision to honor your own word and the understanding that every small step matters. By cultivating discipline, you free yourself from relying on emotions to carry you forward. Instead, you create a consistent, reliable foundation for completing tasks, building confidence with each success.

Completion as a Path to Personal Growth

Finishing what you start doesn't just accomplish a single goal; it transforms you. Each completed task builds confidence, resilience, and a sense of fulfillment. It's an exercise in personal integrity and respect for your own efforts. Moreover, the process of finishing teaches us patience and perseverance—qualities that become assets in every area of life. When we commit to finishing, we become people who can be counted on, both by others and by ourselves.

<u>Real-Life Applications of Rule #12</u>

- **Career Projects:** Break the project into smaller tasks, set milestones with deadlines, and consistently dedicate focused time to each step. Completing the project not only boosts your professional reputation but also demonstrates your ability to follow through under pressure.

- **Fitness Goals:** Focus on incremental progress, such as completing each training session or meal plan. Celebrate small victories along the way, and visualize the sense of accomplishment when you reach your goal. Finishing builds confidence in your ability to sustain positive lifestyle changes.

- **Creative Pursuits:** Commit to a schedule for regular practice or creative work, even if progress feels slow. Remind yourself of the pride you'll feel once the project is complete, and use visualization to push through moments of self-doubt. Completing your creative endeavor reinforces discipline and unlocks your potential for future projects.

<u>Cultivating a Habit of Completion</u>

Make a habit of completion part of your daily life, even in the smallest ways. Finish the book you started, complete the workout you committed to, and tidy up a room until it's done. These small acts reinforce the mindset of finishing and building confidence for larger projects and goals.

<u>Living by Rule #12: Celebrating the Finish Line</u>

When you reach the finish line, take time to celebrate your accomplishment. Recognize the journey, the setbacks you overcame, and the perseverance that brought you here. Let this moment of completion inspire you for future goals, reinforcing your commitment to always finish what you start. Each finish is a stepping stone, building a legacy of resilience and reliability. As you embrace the habit of finishing what you start, you create a life that reflects your dedication, your integrity, and your ability to turn dreams into reality.

Rule #13:
Whatever you do, do it big

The Freedom of Boldness

Life is too short to be lived timidly. **Rule #13 "Whatever you do, do it big"** reminds us to embrace boldness, take risks, and commit to our decisions with conviction. Whether the outcome is a triumph or a misstep, what people remember isn't the result but the courage it took to act. In five years, the details of our choices—whether they were seen as mistakes or strokes of genius—will fade, but the legacy of our bravery and willingness to dream big will endure. This rule challenges us to break free from the fear of failure, trust in the value of taking risks, and live a life rich in experience, growth, and discovery.

Why Bold Choices Matter

Bold choices define who we are and what we stand for. They push us beyond the comfort zone of "what if" into the realm of "why not." Living boldly means acting on our dreams, embracing our goals, and daring to create something extraordinary. The people who inspire us—leaders, artists, and innovators—didn't wait for certainty. They took leaps of faith, accepting the risks of both failure and success. By stepping into boldness, we create a life that reflects our authentic desires and values. Bold decisions bring growth, innovation, and discovery, not because they are always perfect but because they are deliberate steps toward living fully.

The Myth of the "Right" Decision

One of the greatest obstacles to boldness is the belief that there's a single "right" choice. We agonize over decisions, afraid of making a mistake that could set us back. But here's the truth: most choices are just steps along the path, not the path itself. A so-called "wrong" decision can often lead to a better outcome than we ever imagined, and a "right" choice may still involve unexpected setbacks. Life is complex, and our greatest breakthroughs often come from unexpected twists. When we realize there's no perfect decision, we free ourselves to make bolder choices without fear of failure. The key isn't perfection but action. Taking action—especially bold action—gives us the opportunity to shape, learn, and adapt along the way.

Mistakes and Successes Fade—The Experience Remains

Imagine five years from now, looking back on a choice you made today. Chances are, you won't remember every detail, every challenge, or every bit of praise or criticism. What you will remember is the courage it took to make that choice and the way it shaped you. Mistakes, in hindsight, often lose their weight, and the accomplishments we thought were so crucial become milestones on a much longer journey. By doing things "big," you're creating a life rich with experience, not one marked by regret. What endures isn't whether every decision was perfect but the depth, richness, and boldness of the life you created.

Practical Strategies for Living Boldly

1. **Clarify Your Vision and Take Ownership:** Before you act, get clear on what you want and why it matters to you. Bold actions are most effective when they align with your values and goals. Define your vision and make decisions that propel you toward it. When you own your choices, you're more willing to face the risks involved.

2. **Embrace Imperfection and Expect Detours:** Boldness doesn't mean perfection. Understand that mistakes, pivots, and unexpected challenges are part of the process. Treat each setback as an opportunity to learn, refine, and move forward with even greater insight.

3. **Take One Fearless Step at a Time:** You don't have to leap all at once. Take the first small, bold step toward your goal, then the next. Build momentum gradually, and with each step, you'll build confidence, clarity, and resilience.

4. **Develop a "Bounce Back" Mindset:** Boldness requires resilience. Cultivate a mindset that views setbacks as temporary and solvable. When things go wrong, ask yourself, "What's the next best step I can take?" This approach keeps you moving forward, no matter the challenges.

5. **Celebrate Your Boldness, Not Just Your Successes:** Recognize and celebrate each bold choice you make, whether it leads to immediate success or not. Give yourself credit for daring to dream and taking action. The celebration reinforces your commitment to living fully, teaching you to value the journey over the outcome.

<u>Letting Go of What Others Think</u>

One of the most liberating aspects of bold living is realizing that other people's opinions hold little power over your journey. People are often too wrapped up in their own lives to remember the details of your choices, let alone judge them. In five years, most people won't recall if your decision was a wild success or an unexpected setback. The real impact lies in how that choice made you feel, the growth it brought you, and the direction it steered your life. When we stop worrying about the judgments of others, we unlock the freedom to act on what truly matters to us. The courage to live boldly isn't about pleasing others; it's about honoring our unique paths.

The Bold Life: Creating a Legacy of Courage

Living boldly means building a life you're proud of, a life that reflects your true self and your deepest aspirations. Each bold choice creates a legacy—not necessarily of flawless victories but of a life that speaks to your willingness to risk, to try, and to keep going no matter what. This legacy is something far more valuable than a perfect record; it's the story of a life lived fully and without regret. It's a testament to the spirit of resilience, curiosity, and strength that propels you forward, regardless of the outcome.

Real-Life Applications of Rule #13

- **Career Growth:** Instead of hesitating due to fear of failure, step into the challenge with confidence. Lead boldly, take calculated risks, and commit fully to delivering impactful results. Even if the outcome isn't perfect, your willingness to take the leap will set you apart as a visionary leader.

- **Personal Development:** Set ambitious goals and go all in. Share your progress, celebrate milestones, and push beyond what you think is possible. Even if you face setbacks, the process will foster resilience and personal growth.

- **Travel and Life Experiences:** Commit fully to the experience and immerse yourself in it. Take bold steps to embrace the unknown, knowing that the memories, lessons, and growth you gain will far outweigh any temporary uncertainties.

- **Relationship and Connection:** Take the bold step to have the conversation, express your truth, and seek deeper connection. Regardless of the outcome, the act of being genuine and courageous will bring clarity and strengthen your relationships.

Embracing the Journey of Boldness

To do things big is to make each day a statement of courage, creativity, and commitment. Whatever you do, do it with all you have. Be bold enough to stumble, brave enough to keep moving, and resilient enough to laugh in the face of uncertainty. In five years, people may not remember the details of what you did, but they will remember the spirit with which you lived. Embrace that spirit, and let it guide you toward a life that's rich in experiences, lessons, and unforgettable moments. Because, in the end, a life lived boldly is a life truly lived.

Rule #14:
Always deal with the people capable of making the decision (The Follow the Money Rule)

The Value of Direct Access

In the pursuit of any goal—whether personal, professional, or financial—one of the most valuable strategies is to focus your energy and communication on the people who have the authority to make decisions. **Rule #14, also known as the "Follow the Money"** rule, is a reminder to be strategic about whom you engage with, ensuring that your time, resources, and efforts are directed toward individuals who can truly influence outcomes. This rule will explore why it's crucial to identify and work directly with decision-makers, how to recognize when you're dealing with gatekeepers versus true influencers, and strategies for effectively engaging with the right people to reach your goals faster and more efficiently.

Why Working with Decision-Makers Matters

In any system, the people who have the power to make decisions are the ones who shape the outcomes. When we focus on working with decision-makers, we gain direct access to the authority needed to move things forward, make impactful changes, and bring ideas to fruition. Decision-makers have the resources, insights, and influence to open doors, allocate budgets, and create opportunities. Suppose we focus only on those who can offer feedback but lack authority. In that case, we risk becoming caught in cycles of approval and redirection, losing valuable time and potentially stalling our progress. By directing our energy toward people who can say "yes," we minimize delays, cut through unnecessary bureaucracy, and set ourselves up for faster, more effective results.

Recognizing the Decision-Makers

One of the first steps in following this rule is learning to identify who the real decision-makers are. They're not always the people with the loudest voices or the most visible positions, but they are those who have the power to make final calls. In professional settings, decision-makers often hold leadership roles or manage budgets, and they typically have the authority to approve projects, allocate resources, or set strategic direction.

When trying to identify decision-makers, ask yourself:

- **Who ultimately benefits from or is accountable for the decision?** Decision-makers often have a vested interest in the outcome.

- **Who controls the resources or budget?** Financial influence often accompanies decision-making power, especially in organizational settings.

- **Who has the authority to override or fast-track decisions?** Decision-makers can typically bypass or streamline processes when needed.

Once you can accurately pinpoint the key decision-makers, you'll be able to focus your efforts on establishing a direct and meaningful connection with them.

Avoiding the Gatekeeper Trap

Gatekeepers often play a necessary role in organizational structures, controlling access to decision-makers and managing information flow. However, it's essential to recognize when you're dealing with a gatekeeper versus a true influencer. Engaging only with gatekeepers may lead to delays, as they often lack the authority to make final decisions.

When interacting with gatekeepers, it's important to be polite and respectful while also communicating your intention to reach those who can make decisions. Asking direct but courteous questions—like, "Who would be the best person to discuss this proposal with?" or "Could you connect me with the person overseeing this decision?"—can help you navigate past the gatekeepers without alienating them.

Practical Strategies for Reaching Decision-Makers

1. **Do Your Homework:** Before reaching out, research the organization's structure and identify the key players involved. LinkedIn, company websites, and industry networks are valuable resources for understanding who holds authority. The more you know about a decision maker's role, background, and current goals, the better positioned you are to make a compelling and relevant case for why your proposal or idea deserves their attention.

2. **Make Your Pitch Relevant to Their Interests and Goals:** Decision-makers are more likely to listen when they see the value in what you're proposing. Tailor your pitch to align with their goals and interests, addressing how your proposal meets their strategic priorities or solves a problem they care about. By demonstrating that you understand their perspective, you're more likely to capture their attention and support.

3. **Build a Network of Advocates:** Sometimes, direct access to decision-makers isn't immediately possible. In these cases, building relationships with people who have influence and connections can help you gain access. Cultivate allies who can vouch for your credibility, advocate for your ideas, and facilitate introductions to decision-makers. A well-connected network can provide invaluable support as you work your way up.

4. **Use Direct Communication Channels:** Email, LinkedIn messages, and professional networking events offer opportunities to communicate directly with decision-makers. Craft clear, concise messages that respect their time, highlighting the value you bring and why your proposal matters. A well-structured, respectful message increases the likelihood of a positive response and establishes you as someone who respects their time and priorities.

5. **Demonstrate Patience and Professionalism:** Dealing with decision-makers often requires patience. Even when you have direct access, decision-making processes can take time. Remain professional, be willing to follow up politely, and show persistence without coming across as overly demanding. Patience combined with consistent communication can build respect and improve your chances of a favorable outcome.

Handling Rejections and Redirections

Not every interaction with a decision-maker will lead to an immediate "yes." Sometimes, they may reject your proposal or suggest an alternative approach. Rather than viewing rejection as a setback, treat it as an opportunity to gain insights and improve your approach. Ask for feedback on how you could strengthen your proposal or better align it with their goals. Being willing to adapt based on feedback shows resilience and professionalism, traits that decision-makers respect. Moreover, a respectful response to rejection keeps the door open for future opportunities, reinforcing your reputation as someone who values constructive collaboration.

The Power of Respect and Accountability

Decision-makers appreciate those who respect their authority and come prepared. When you approach a decision-maker with a clear understanding of their priorities, a well-thought-out proposal, and respect for their time, you're positioning yourself as a valuable asset rather than a mere petitioner. This approach not only increases your chances of a positive outcome but also establishes a foundation of mutual respect. Accountability is equally crucial. If a decision-maker supports your proposal, it's essential to follow through and deliver results. Fulfilling your commitments demonstrates reliability and strengthens your professional credibility, making decision-makers more likely to support you again in the future.

Real-Life Applications of Rule #14

- **Career Advancement:** Instead of only discussing your aspirations with colleagues or middle managers, schedule a meeting with decision-makers like your department head or HR director. Present your case clearly, focusing on how your skills align with the organization's goals, ensuring your request reaches someone with the authority to act.

- **Conflict Resolution:** Engage directly with city council members, policymakers, or other officials who have the authority to implement change. Present a well-prepared case that highlights community benefits to increase the likelihood of action.

- **Networking for Opportunities:** Instead of solely networking at peer levels, target industry leaders, recruiters, or professionals with decision-making influence. Engage with them through direct communication channels like LinkedIn or professional events.

- **Travel and Hospitality:** Request to speak with a supervisor or manager who has the authority to resolve your issue immediately rather than wasting time with representatives who may lack decision-making power.

Building a Legacy of Strategic Engagement

Following the "Follow the Money" rule doesn't just help you reach your immediate goals—it's a principle that builds a legacy of strategic thinking and purposeful engagement. By focusing on decision-makers, you're choosing to work efficiently, valuing your own time as well as others. This approach enables you to make an impact, build valuable connections, and establish a reputation for effectiveness. When you consistently prioritize dealing with decision-makers, you're creating a career and life based on intentionality. You're not merely reacting to circumstances; you're proactively shaping your path, choosing to engage with those who have the power to create real change.

Embracing the Follow the Money Rule in Life

Rule #14 reminds us to be mindful of where we invest our time and energy. By engaging with decision-makers, we're not just pursuing our goals; we're learning to value efficiency, impact, and the art of meaningful communication. This rule encourages us to see each interaction as an opportunity to create positive outcomes, both for ourselves and for those who support us. In life, as in business, decision-makers often shape our most significant opportunities. By identifying and connecting with those who can influence our path, we're embracing our power to create a life that reflects our ambitions, dreams, and highest potential. Whether in work, relationships, or personal projects, Rule #14 empowers us to move forward with clarity and purpose, always guided by the wisdom of choosing to follow the people—and paths—that truly matter.

Rule #15:
Negotiate from positions of strength

The Power of Strong Negotiation

Negotiation is an art that goes beyond merely seeking agreement; it's about creating an exchange that benefits everyone involved while ensuring that your needs, values, and objectives are fully recognized. **Rule #15 "Negotiate from Positions of Strength"** reminds us that successful negotiation is rooted in self-assurance, preparation, and a clear understanding of our worth. When we negotiate from a place of strength, we increase the likelihood of achieving outcomes that reflect our goals and respect our boundaries. In this rule, we'll explore the foundations of negotiating with strength, why confidence and preparation matter, and how to create the conditions that position you as an equal and respected partner in any negotiation.

The Foundations of Strength in Negotiation

Strength in negotiation isn't about overpowering or manipulating the other party; it's about understanding your value and asserting it with preparation and clarity. Negotiating from a position of strength involves entering the conversation with a clear understanding of what you bring to the table, what you need in return, and what you're willing to compromise on. This approach allows you to engage with confidence and prevents you from feeling pressured into agreeing to terms that don't align with your interests. The foundation of negotiating from strength lies in self-knowledge—being clear about your goals, limits, and non-negotiables. It also requires thorough preparation, including gathering relevant information, planning strategically, and projecting confidence, even when the negotiation feels intimidating. By incorporating these elements, you not only increase your chances of achieving a favorable outcome but also earn respect and credibility from the other party.

The Role of Preparation in Building Strength

Preparation is one of the most powerful ways to build strength in negotiation. When you've done your homework, you feel equipped to engage confidently and respond thoughtfully. Effective preparation involves understanding both your position and the position of the other party, including the factors that influence their goals, challenges, and potential areas of flexibility. Key aspects of preparation include setting clear objectives, which means defining exactly what you want to achieve, whether it's a specific salary, better working conditions, or a fairer contract. Clear objectives keep you focused and help you avoid getting sidetracked.

Additionally, researching market and industry standards is essential; knowing relevant benchmarks or data ensures you're informed and able to advocate effectively for your value. For example, if you're negotiating a salary, understanding the industry average for your role helps you position yourself appropriately. Lastly, identifying your BATNA (Best Alternative to a Negotiated Agreement) gives you a solid backup plan, reducing pressure to accept unfavorable terms and bolstering your confidence. Thorough preparation not only reinforces your value but also positions you as a knowledgeable and credible negotiator.

The Confidence Factor

Confidence is the bridge that connects preparation with success in negotiation. It signals that you understand your worth, have carefully considered your position, and are ready to advocate for yourself. Confidence is not about arrogance; it's about calmly and clearly expressing your needs while respecting the perspective of the other party. You can cultivate confidence by practicing your pitch and rehearsing how you'll present your points to ensure clarity and assertiveness. The more you practice, the more natural and poised you'll feel during the actual conversation. Body language also plays a crucial role—sitting or standing tall, maintaining steady eye contact, and using calm, deliberate gestures convey assurance, even if you feel nervous inside.

Additionally, focusing on facts rather than emotions helps solidify your confidence. Citing objective information, such as industry standards or your unique qualifications, reinforces your preparedness and professionalism. When you project confidence, you invite respect and increase the likelihood that your terms will be taken seriously.

Practical Strategies for Negotiating from Positions of Strength

1. **Anchor with a Strong Opening:** Begin the negotiation by clearly and confidently stating your initial position. This sets the tone and anchors the conversation around your goals. Opening with strength shows that you're prepared and committed to reaching a favorable outcome, helping you establish credibility from the outset.

2. **Ask Open-Ended Questions to Understand Their Position:** Strong negotiators don't just talk; they listen. Ask open-ended questions that allow the other party to share their priorities, constraints, and objectives. Understanding their needs can reveal areas of common ground or potential compromises, which strengthens your own negotiating position.

3. **Stay Focused on Value, Not Just Price:** Whether you're negotiating a salary or a contract, emphasize the value you bring to the table, not just the numbers. Articulate how your skills, experience, or unique contributions align with the goals of the other party. This approach allows you to negotiate from a place of value, making it easier to justify your terms.

4. **Know When to Pause and Reflect:** Silence can be a powerful negotiation tool. After making a key point or counteroffer, pause and give the other party space to respond. This not only signals confidence but also prevents you from over-explaining or backtracking on your position. The pause invites them to consider your terms seriously.

5. **Be Willing to Walk Away:** The ultimate strength in negotiation is the ability to walk away if terms don't align with your needs or values. Knowing your boundaries and being willing to step back shows that you're not desperate, and it signals that you respect yourself enough to pursue only what's fair. Sometimes, walking away can even prompt the other party to reconsider and return with better terms.

<u>Navigating Difficult Moments with Grace</u>

Negotiation can become tense, especially when the stakes are high. However, even during challenging moments, strength in negotiation is about maintaining grace and respect. Remember that disagreements are natural, and maintaining a calm, professional demeanor helps keep the conversation constructive.

If you encounter resistance, return to the facts and reinforce your value. Avoid taking counterarguments personally and instead use them as opportunities to understand the other party's needs better. Responding gracefully, even in difficult moments, strengthens your position and reflects positively on your character.

<u>Real-Life Applications of Rule #15</u>

- **Salary and Benefits Negotiation:** Research industry standards for your role, document your accomplishments and highlight how your skills align with company goals. Present your case confidently, including specific figures and examples of your contributions, to secure favorable terms.

- **Contract Negotiations:** Define your non-negotiables, such as payment terms or project scope, and prepare examples of past successes to demonstrate your value. Negotiate from a place of professionalism and clarity, emphasizing the quality and reliability you bring to the partnership.

- **Dispute Resolution:** Focus on facts and shared goals rather than emotions. Clearly articulate your perspective and suggest solutions that align with both parties' interests, negotiating a fair resolution from a position of calm authority.

Creating a Legacy of Strong Negotiation

Negotiating from positions of strength isn't just about reaching favorable outcomes in individual situations; it's about creating a legacy of respect, professionalism, and self-assurance. When you consistently approach negotiation with clarity, confidence, and a focus on value, you build a reputation as someone who knows their worth and communicates it effectively. This approach has lasting benefits beyond any single negotiation. It shapes how people perceive you, fosters mutual respect in your professional and personal relationships, and creates opportunities that align with your true value. The legacy of strong negotiation is a life where you're respected, heard, and valued, both by others and by yourself.

Embracing Negotiation as an Empowering Skill

Negotiating from a position of strength is more than a rule—it's an empowering mindset that influences how you approach life. When you know your worth, prepare thoroughly, and communicate confidently, you're setting a standard for how you expect to be treated. This skill is a cornerstone of self-respect and personal empowerment, reminding you that your needs and goals are worthy of pursuit. Whether you're negotiating a major career move, a partnership, or a personal commitment, embracing this rule helps you navigate with clarity and purpose. Each time you negotiate from a place of strength, you're reinforcing the belief that your value deserves recognition—and that is a power that can positively impact every area of your life.

Rule #16:
People do what is inspected, not expected

The Power of Accountability

In life, we often assume that our expectations will naturally lead to desired outcomes—that people will rise to the occasion simply because they know what we want. **Rule #16 "People Do What Is Inspected, Not Expected"** reminds us that expectations alone are not enough to drive consistent results. To achieve reliable outcomes, we need to follow up, offer support, and create accountability actively. This rule is about building systems of accountability that encourage follow-through, consistency, and clarity in our interactions with others. Whether we're working with teams, guiding others, or managing our personal goals, regular inspection is key to creating lasting impact.

Why Inspection Matters More Than Expectation

Expectations are important; they set the foundation for what we hope to achieve. However, without reinforcement, expectations can become vague, easily misunderstood, or deprioritized. When people know that someone will check in on their progress, they are more likely to stay committed, attentive, and accountable. Consider a workplace where a manager sets clear expectations but never follows up. Employees may initially strive to meet these standards, but over time, without reinforcement, priorities may shift, and standards can slip. By contrast, when the manager regularly checks in, offers feedback, and reinforces the goals, employees feel more motivated to stay on track. Inspection doesn't mean micromanaging or constant surveillance. Instead, it's about creating a structured system of follow-up that encourages accountability and supports individuals in reaching their goals.

Building a Culture of Accountability

Accountability is the backbone of effective teams, relationships, and personal growth. When people know that their actions will be reviewed, they're more likely to perform at their best. Inspection also creates a culture of transparency and trust, where expectations are reinforced with supportive check-ins rather than left as abstract hopes. Creating accountability is a shared responsibility. It benefits both the person setting expectations and those working to meet them. Accountability provides clarity, direction, and feedback, which help people understand where they stand and how they can improve. When inspection becomes a regular practice, it fosters an environment where people are motivated to meet standards and feel supported in their efforts.

Practical Strategies for Implementing Inspection

1. **Set Clear, Measurable Goals:** Vague expectations are difficult to inspect. Make sure your goals are specific, measurable, and time-bound so that both you and others know exactly what's expected. For example, instead of setting a goal to "improve communication," a clear objective would be to "provide weekly updates on project progress." Clarity ensures that expectations are actionable and makes inspection straightforward.

2. **Schedule Regular Check-Ins:** Inspection is most effective when it's consistent. Set up regular check-ins to discuss progress, address challenges, and provide feedback. For a team, this might mean weekly meetings, while for personal goals, it could mean self-reflection or accountability partnerships. Regular check-ins prevent issues from escalating and offer opportunities for course correction along the way.

3. **Provide Constructive Feedback:** Inspection should be a positive and growth-oriented experience, not a source of criticism. Offer feedback that acknowledges achievements and gently highlights areas for improvement. Constructive feedback shows that you're invested in the other person's success and encourages them to keep striving for their best.

4. **Celebrate Milestones and Progress:** Recognizing and celebrating progress is a powerful way to reinforce accountability. When people see that their hard work is noticed and valued, they're more motivated to continue. Celebrating milestones, no matter how small, shows that inspection isn't just about oversight—it's about valuing commitment and consistency.

5. **Hold Yourself Accountable, Too:** Lead by example by inspecting your own commitments. If you set an expectation for yourself, follow through by tracking your own progress and celebrating your wins. When others see you holding yourself accountable, they're more likely to feel inspired to do the same.

<u>Applying the Rule to Self-Improvement</u>

This rule doesn't just apply to managing others; it's also essential for self-discipline. When it comes to personal goals, we often set high expectations for ourselves but struggle to stay accountable without a system of inspection. By establishing regular checkpoints—whether through journaling, self-reflection, or a personal accountability partner—you can create a structure that keeps you on track.

For example, if you have a goal to exercise regularly, inspecting your progress might mean tracking your workouts in a journal or app and reviewing your achievements each week. When you inspect your own progress, you're more likely to stay motivated, and you'll also develop a better understanding of what helps you stay consistent.

Avoiding Micromanagement

One important distinction to make is between inspection and micromanagement. While inspection involves setting clear expectations and regularly checking in, micromanagement involves excessive control and constant monitoring. Micromanagement stifles autonomy and can lead to frustration and disengagement.

The goal of inspection is to provide support, not to monitor every detail. When done respectfully, inspection offers a framework that empowers people to meet their goals without feeling restricted. In relationships or teams, effective inspection is based on trust, open communication, and a shared commitment to improvement.

Building Trust Through Transparency

When people know that their progress will be inspected, it creates a transparent environment where expectations are clear, feedback is regular, and everyone understands the value of their work. Inspection builds trust by ensuring that no one is left in the dark about what's expected of them or how they're doing.

Transparency in inspection also gives people a sense of security, as they know they'll have the chance to receive feedback and address any issues before they become problems. This trust empowers individuals to ask for help if needed and to feel confident that their efforts are being recognized.

Practical Examples of Inspection in Action

- **In the Workplace**: A manager sets quarterly goals for each team member and schedules monthly check-ins to discuss progress. During these check-ins, they review specific achievements, provide feedback on areas for improvement, and offer support to address any obstacles. Team members know their work is valued and have clear guidance on how to succeed.

- **In Personal Goals**: Someone aiming to improve their health starts tracking their meals and exercise. Every week, they review their progress, assess areas for improvement, and set small goals for the following week. This regular inspection keeps them motivated and allows them to make gradual, sustainable progress.

- **In Relationships**: A couple sets a goal to improve communication by having a weekly "check-in" conversation. During this time, they share any thoughts, challenges, or appreciations they've experienced. This regular practice fosters open dialogue and ensures that small issues don't go unaddressed.

The Long-Term Benefits of Inspection

People rise to the occasion when they know their efforts will be recognized, appreciated, and valued. By creating systems of inspection, you're cultivating a culture of accountability, clarity, and mutual respect. Inspection fosters an environment where people feel secure in their goals, supported in their efforts, and connected to a shared purpose. Over time, regular inspection creates habits of consistency and self-discipline, making it easier for everyone involved to meet expectations and exceed them. This habit of inspecting progress leads to reliable results, continuous improvement, and a sense of accomplishment for everyone involved.

Embracing the Power of Accountability

Living by Rule #16 is about more than just achieving goals; it's about respecting the power of accountability to create meaningful, lasting results. When we inspect what matters to us, we're choosing to engage thoughtfully, to support others fully, and to make progress a consistent part of our journey. In the end, people do what is inspected, not expected, because inspection shows that their work, their efforts, and their growth are worth noticing. By embracing this rule, we're choosing to create a life of purpose, clarity, and commitment—one where expectations become realities, goals turn into achievements, and everyone is empowered to be their best.

Rule #17:
Battle dishonesty with truth

The Power of Truth

Dishonesty—whether it's in personal relationships, professional settings, or even within ourselves—can create a tangled web of mistrust, confusion, and negativity. **Rule #17, "Battle Dishonesty with Truth,"** is a reminder of the incredible power of truth to cut through deception, build trust, and bring clarity to any situation. In a world where dishonesty can sometimes feel pervasive, truth is our strongest defense, a means to protect our integrity and honor our values. This rule explores how truth serves as a foundation for resilience, connection, and self-respect. By choosing truth over deceit, we not only challenge dishonesty but also create an environment where transparency, respect, and authenticity can flourish.

The Role of Truth in Confronting Dishonesty

Dishonesty erodes trust, damages relationships, and creates an environment of uncertainty. When dishonesty goes unchecked, it can lead to misunderstandings, poor decisions, and unnecessary conflict. By responding to dishonesty with truth, we're choosing a path of clarity and accountability. Truth, however, isn't just about correcting others. It's also about embodying honesty in our own actions setting a standard that encourages others to act with integrity. Battling dishonesty with truth means choosing to face difficult situations with courage, resisting the urge to retaliate with lies or half-truths, and remaining rooted in our commitment to transparency.

Why Truth Is the Ultimate Equalizer

Truth is a grounding force. It doesn't require embellishment, justification, or manipulation; it simply is. In contrast, dishonesty often requires layers of deception, creating a fragile foundation that eventually collapses under scrutiny. Truth has a way of revealing itself, bringing stability and consistency to situations clouded by dishonesty. Think of truth as a compass that guides us through complex interactions. When we approach situations with honesty, we invite others to do the same. Truth fosters mutual respect, enabling open dialogue and leading to genuine understanding, even in challenging moments.

Choosing Truth Over Retaliation

When we're faced with dishonesty, the temptation to retaliate with deception can be strong. But battling dishonesty with more dishonesty only fuels mistrust and complicates the situation further. Instead, responding with truth disarms dishonesty by removing its power. Truth sheds light on deception, revealing intentions, actions, and motivations with clarity. Imagine someone spreading a false rumor about you at work. Responding with a calm, truthful account of the situation not only discredits the rumor but also reinforces your integrity. By sticking to the truth, you maintain your credibility and avoid stooping to the level of dishonesty, showing others that you can rise above it.

Practical Strategies for Battling Dishonesty with Truth

1. **Stay Calm and Centered:** Dishonesty can provoke frustration and anger. Before responding, take a moment to breathe and center yourself. Responding from a place of calm allows you to present the truth with clarity rather than emotion, preventing the situation from escalating.

2. **Stick to the Facts:** When addressing dishonesty, focus on factual details rather than interpretations or assumptions. By sticking to what you know to be true, you avoid getting drawn into unnecessary arguments or speculation. Facts create a strong, indisputable foundation that others can trust.

3. **Use "I" Statements:** Instead of accusing others, which can trigger defensiveness, use "I" statements to communicate your perspective honestly. For instance, say, "I feel concerned about this because..." instead of "You're lying." This approach encourages open dialogue and makes it easier for others to respond truthfully.

4. **Set Boundaries to Protect Your Integrity:** In situations where dishonesty persists, it may be necessary to set boundaries. Let others know that while you value honesty, you won't engage in conversations that are not based on truth. This reinforces your commitment to integrity and discourages dishonest behavior.

5. **Seek Resolution, Not Revenge:** When dealing with dishonesty, aim to resolve the situation rather than retaliate. Ask questions, clarify misunderstandings, and listen to the other person's perspective. Truth isn't about winning an argument; it's about creating mutual understanding and finding a way forward.

The Importance of Self-Honesty

Battling dishonesty with truth isn't only about addressing external deception; it's also about confronting any dishonesty within ourselves. Self-honesty is the foundation of personal growth, as it requires us to face our flaws, accept responsibility, and acknowledge uncomfortable truths about ourselves. When we are honest with ourselves, we become more confident and authentic, knowing that our actions align with our values. Self-honesty also makes it easier to confront dishonesty in others, as our own inner conflicts do not weigh us down. By practicing self-honesty, we reinforce our commitment to truth in all areas of life, creating a strong, consistent character.

Truth as a Catalyst for Positive Change

Truth can be uncomfortable, but it's also the catalyst for genuine change. When dishonesty is met with truth, it challenges the status quo, prompting self-reflection and accountability. Truth can disrupt comfort zones, forcing people to confront their actions and consider new perspectives. Truth fosters growth by creating transparency, which leads to accountability. When we respond to dishonesty with honesty, we're offering others an opportunity to reflect on their actions and, if willing, make amends. This transparency not only promotes resolution but also strengthens relationships based on trust and mutual respect.

Leading by Example

Responding to dishonesty with truth is also about setting an example for others. When we choose truth over deception, we're showing others the strength of integrity, even in difficult situations. This example can have a powerful impact, encouraging others to act honestly and creating an environment where dishonesty is discouraged. In a leadership context, for instance, choosing transparency and honesty builds trust among team members. When people see a leader address challenges truthfully, they feel safer to be open and honest themselves, knowing that honesty is valued and respected.

Practical Scenarios of Battling Dishonesty with Truth

- **In Personal Relationships**: If a friend tells a white lie that bothers you, gently address it with honesty. Explain how the lie affected you and express your preference for transparency, even if the truth may be uncomfortable. This approach reinforces trust and sets a precedent for honesty in the relationship.

- **In Professional Settings**: If a colleague presents misleading information, calmly clarify the facts in a way that focuses on accuracy rather than accusation. For example, "Actually, the report shows that…" rather than "You're wrong." By focusing on facts, you maintain professionalism while addressing dishonesty.

- **Within Yourself**: When you notice yourself avoiding a difficult truth, take a moment to reflect. Acknowledge why you may be hesitant to face the truth and remind yourself that self-honesty is essential for growth. Embrace the truth, even if it's challenging, as a way to build resilience and authenticity.

The Freedom That Comes with Truth

Truth liberates us from the complexities of dishonesty. It provides a sense of clarity and inner peace, knowing that we're acting in alignment with our values. When we consistently respond to dishonesty with truth, we're choosing to live authentically, free from the weight of deceit or hidden agendas. Battling dishonesty with truth not only resolves conflict but also protects our integrity and reputation. It establishes us as people who value honesty and transparency, individuals who can be trusted to act in good faith. This freedom empowers us to build relationships and pursue goals with confidence, knowing that our character speaks for itself.

Living a Life Anchored in Truth

Living by Rule #17 is a choice to embody integrity, resilience, and compassion. Truth becomes not just a tool for addressing dishonesty but a way of life that honors both ourselves and those we encounter. When we battle dishonesty with truth, we create a foundation of trust, respect, and accountability that enriches our lives and the lives of those around us. In the end, truth is more than just a response to dishonesty; it's a commitment to live with purpose, clarity, and integrity. Embracing this rule empowers us to navigate life's challenges with unwavering authenticity, leaving a legacy of honesty and respect that speaks louder than words.

Rule #18:

Do not ask others what you are not prepared to do yourself

The Integrity of Leading by Example

In every area of life—whether in our careers, relationships, or personal goals—there's immense value in embodying the standards we set for others. **Rule #18, "Do Not Ask Others What You Are Not Prepared to Do Yourself,"** is about practicing integrity and setting an example that earns respect. It's a reminder that true leadership and influence come not from demanding but from demonstrating. When we lead by example, we foster trust, inspire motivation, and build stronger, more authentic connections. This rule explores how aligning our words and actions enhances our credibility, strengthens relationships, and creates a positive impact on those around us. By committing to do ourselves what we ask of others, we create a foundation of respect and authenticity that drives real progress.

Why Leading by Example Matters

There's a natural instinct in people to mirror what they see, and actions often speak louder than words. When others see that we're willing to put in the effort, take on challenges, and follow through on the same standards we set, they're more likely to follow suit. Conversely, if we set expectations for others that we don't uphold ourselves, we risk losing credibility and trust. Leading by example creates alignment between what we say and what we do, eliminating the gap between expectation and action. It fosters a culture of accountability, mutual respect, and shared effort. When we demonstrate our willingness to do what we ask of others, we're not only setting a standard but also empowering those around us to rise to their potential.

The Importance of Consistency in Integrity

Integrity is about consistency—consistently acting in alignment with our values and maintaining the same standards for ourselves as we do for others. When we hold ourselves accountable to the same expectations, we build a reputation of fairness and reliability. People are more likely to respect and support someone who practices what they preach. For instance, if a manager asks their team to meet tight deadlines but consistently fails to meet their own commitments, the team's respect and motivation will likely decrease. However, when a leader meets deadlines, helps during crunch times, and supports the team under pressure, they create a culture of shared responsibility. This consistency in integrity not only earns respect but also motivates others to contribute their best.

Practical Strategies for Leading by Example

1. **Set Standards for Yourself First:** Before setting expectations for others, ensure you're upholding those standards in your own actions. Whether it's punctuality, professionalism, or effort, make sure you're consistently modeling the behavior you'd like to see in others. If you expect accountability, demonstrate accountability in your commitments and actions.

2. **Be Transparent About Your Efforts:** Let others see the work you're putting in. If you're asking for extra effort on a project, share what you're doing to contribute. This transparency shows that you're not just delegating but actively working alongside others, fostering a sense of shared purpose.

3. **Admit Mistakes and Take Responsibility:** If you fall short of your own standards, acknowledge it openly. Taking responsibility for your mistakes demonstrates humility and integrity. This openness encourages others to do the same, creating a culture where people feel safe, to be honest and accountable.

4. **Demonstrate Willingness to Support Others:** When you ask others to take on a task, be ready to lend a hand if needed. This doesn't mean you must always do the task yourself but be willing to step in or support as needed. Knowing that you're prepared to help reinforces your commitment to the team's success.

5. **Practice Empathy in Your Expectations:** Consider the effort, time, and challenges involved in any task before asking others to take it on. Ask yourself, "Would I be willing to do this under these circumstances?" If the answer is no, it may be worth reevaluating the request. Empathy ensures that your expectations are fair and realistic.

The Impact of Hypocrisy on Relationships

When we set expectations for others that we're unwilling to meet ourselves, it creates an unspoken tension. People are perceptive; they can sense hypocrisy, and when they feel that they're being held to double standards, trust is eroded. Hypocrisy can lead to resentment, disengagement, and a breakdown in communication, as people may feel that they're being asked to meet unrealistic or unfair expectations. True leadership requires self-awareness. By being mindful of our actions, we avoid the trap of hypocrisy and create a culture of trust and respect. People are more willing to invest in relationships where they feel valued and treated equitably.

Building a Culture of Mutual Respect

When we commit to doing what we ask of others, we're not just building respect for ourselves; we're creating an environment where respect flows both ways. A culture of mutual respect is one where everyone feels valued, and as a result, people are more willing to go the extra mile, collaborate openly, and support one another. Imagine a workplace where team members see their leaders actively participating, understanding their challenges, and providing support when needed. This culture inspires individuals to step up, take initiative, and give their best. The same principle applies in personal relationships; when both parties practice what they ask of each other, they build a bond grounded in trust and mutual admiration.

Practical Applications in Everyday Scenarios

- **In the Workplace**: If you're a manager, ask yourself if you're meeting the same standards you set for your team. Are you delivering on time, being responsive, and showing up prepared? By modeling these behaviors, you create an environment where everyone is motivated to match your commitment.

- **In Personal Relationships**: If you expect honesty, kindness, or understanding from others, make sure you're offering those qualities in return. For example, if you ask your partner to communicate openly, ensure that you're also sharing your thoughts and listening actively. Mutual respect fosters a stronger, more balanced relationship.

- **In Personal Growth**: When setting personal goals, hold yourself to the same standards you would set for others. If you believe in the importance of self-care or continuous learning, prioritize these areas in your own life. This alignment strengthens your self-respect and reinforces the principle of leading by example.

Overcoming Challenges in Leading by Example

Leading by example isn't always easy; it requires self-discipline, humility, and resilience. There may be times when you feel stretched or challenged to meet your own expectations, but these moments offer opportunities for growth. When you encounter difficulty, remember that leading by example is about progress, not perfection. Acknowledge the effort, celebrate the small wins, and stay committed to embodying the standards you set. Being prepared to do what you ask of others doesn't mean you must be flawless; it means demonstrating integrity even when the path is challenging. This commitment builds resilience and strengthens your influence, helping you navigate obstacles with credibility and purpose.

Creating a Legacy of Integrity

When you consistently practice Rule #18, you're creating a legacy of integrity. You're demonstrating to others that you are someone who stands by your word, someone who is willing to put in the work and support those around you. This legacy endures beyond individual interactions, shaping how people perceive you and inspiring them to live with the same commitment to authenticity. A legacy of integrity creates a ripple effect, encouraging others to lead by example and treat each other with respect and fairness. Whether in the workplace, community, or family, this approach leaves a lasting impact, fostering a culture where everyone feels valued and motivated to contribute their best.

Embracing Rule #18 in Everyday Life

Living by Rule #18 is a commitment to embodying your values, building trust, and leading with humility. When you ask others to do something, remember that your willingness to do it yourself sets the tone. This rule reminds us that actions have a profound impact, that true leadership is grounded in empathy and respect, and that by aligning our words and deeds, we can inspire and empower those around us. In the end, Rule #18 is more than just a guideline—it's a way of life that creates deeper, more authentic relationships, builds respect, and enriches both your personal and professional worlds. By embracing this rule, you're choosing to live with integrity, authenticity, and purpose, setting a powerful example that resonates far beyond words.

Rule #19:
Just because you can, doesn't mean you should

The Wisdom of Discernment

In a world that often equates capability with action, **Rule #19 "Just Because You Can, Doesn't Mean You Should"** reminds us that not every opportunity or impulse deserves our energy. Knowing what you're capable of and knowing when to act on that capability are two different things. This rule is about practicing discernment, setting boundaries, and understanding that restraint is sometimes the wisest choice. Living by this principle means learning to evaluate the potential impact of our actions, choosing intentionally rather than impulsively. By doing so, we create space for what truly matters, conserve our energy, and act with purpose. This rule explores how to practice discernment, recognize when not to act, and understand that wisdom often lies in knowing when to say "no."

The Power of Choosing Wisely

In life, we're faced with countless choices, and sometimes, the temptation to act just because we can is strong. The ability to say "yes" to everything—whether it's taking on more responsibilities, expressing every opinion, or pursuing every opportunity—can be alluring. Still, it often leads to exhaustion, distraction, and even regret. Choosing wisely is about quality over quantity, focusing on actions that align with our values, priorities, and goals. Just because we have the skills or resources to take on a new project doesn't mean it's the best use of our time. Just because we can win an argument doesn't mean it's worth the emotional energy. By learning to say "no" to the unnecessary, we open up our lives for the meaningful, reducing stress and increasing fulfillment.

Recognizing the Difference Between "Can" and "Should"

The difference between "can" and "should" lies in intention and impact. While "can" speaks to capability, "should" focuses on purpose and alignment. Before taking action, it's important to reflect on key questions to guide your decision-making. Ask yourself: What's the purpose behind this action? Is it to fulfill a genuine need, serve a meaningful goal, or simply because you feel capable of doing it? Consider whether the action aligns with your values and contributes to the life you want to build or the person you aim to become. Lastly, evaluate the potential consequences—how might this choice affect your time, energy, relationships, or well-being? By thoughtfully answering these questions, you can gain clarity on whether an action is truly worth pursuing or better left undone. This discernment helps you act with intention, ensuring your choices add value to your life and positively impact those around you.

Practicing Restraint as a Form of Strength

In a culture that often celebrates action and achievement, restraint is a rarely acknowledged but powerful strength. Choosing not to act—whether it's resisting an argument, declining an extra responsibility, or holding back from sharing an opinion—requires self-control and a clear sense of priorities. Imagine being in a meeting where a colleague says something that isn't entirely accurate. While you might have the knowledge to correct them, doing so could disrupt the conversation, damage your relationship, or sidetrack the meeting. Practicing restraint at this moment, choosing not to act just because you can, demonstrates maturity and emotional intelligence. Restraint is not about passivity; it's about exercising conscious choice. By mastering restraint, we're choosing to conserve our energy for actions that truly matter, fostering a life of purpose and focus.

Practical Strategies for Practicing Discernment

1. **Pause Before Acting:** When faced with an impulse or opportunity, take a moment to pause and reflect. This simple act of slowing down allows you to consider whether the action aligns with your goals or values. Pausing helps prevent knee-jerk reactions and encourages mindful choices.

2. **Evaluate Your Energy and Resources:** Consider whether you have the mental, emotional, or physical resources to take on an action. If you're already stretched thin, adding more can lead to burnout. Learn to say "no" to what's unnecessary or unsustainable, and reserve your energy for the pursuits that truly resonate.

3. **Seek Alignment with Long-Term Goals:** Before committing to an action, ask yourself if it supports your long-term goals. If the action doesn't contribute to the bigger picture of what you want to achieve, it might be best left undone. Alignment with long-term goals ensures that each decision moves you closer to a meaningful outcome.

4. **Use Empathy to Guide Your Choices:** Just because you have the power to do or say something doesn't mean it's kind or beneficial for others. Consider how your actions might affect others. Practicing empathy in decision-making helps you navigate situations with sensitivity and respect, strengthening your relationships.

5. **Set Boundaries and Stick to Them:** Boundaries are essential for discerning when to act and when to hold back. Establish clear boundaries for what you will and won't take on, and honor these limits. Setting boundaries allows you to avoid overcommitting, ensuring that your actions are intentional and in line with your priorities.

When "Can" Leads to Regret

At times, saying "yes" simply because we can lead to regret or dissatisfaction. Perhaps we take on a project we're not passionate about, agree to a social commitment we're too tired to attend or give feedback when it isn't needed. These moments can leave us feeling drained, stressed, or out of alignment with our true selves. Learning to recognize these situations and adjust our behavior prevents regret from becoming a recurring pattern. Each time we choose to act intentionally rather than impulsively, we're reinforcing our commitment to a more meaningful, focused life.

The Importance of Self-Control

Self-control is the foundation of discernment. Without self-control, we're more likely to act on impulse, saying "yes" to everything or reacting without considering the consequences. Self-control helps us navigate the difference between capability and purpose, grounding us in our values rather than fleeting desires. Developing self-control doesn't mean suppressing your capabilities or desires; it means directing them with purpose. When you cultivate self-control, you're more equipped to make decisions that serve your long-term happiness and well-being.

Practical Scenarios of "Just Because You Can, Doesn't Mean You Should"

- **In Professional Settings**: Imagine you have the skills to take on an additional project, but doing so would spread you thin and impact your existing commitments. Recognizing that your time is limited, you might choose to decline the project, focusing on delivering excellence in your current role instead.

- **In Relationships**: Let's say you notice a flaw in a friend's approach to a problem. While you might have the insight to point it out, it's important to consider if unsolicited advice would be helpful or if it might strain the relationship. Sometimes, holding back and offering support rather than advice is the wiser choice.

- **In Personal Development**: You may have the financial means to buy something extravagant, but that doesn't necessarily mean it will bring you lasting joy or align with your values. Practicing discernment in spending ensures that your resources are directed toward what truly enhances your life.

Embracing Freedom Through Discernment

When we adopt the mindset of "just because you can, doesn't mean you should," we're giving ourselves the freedom to live intentionally without the pressure to say "yes" to everything. This freedom allows us to focus on what brings meaning, fulfillment, and balance, helping us avoid the stress and distraction that comes from overcommitting or acting impulsively. Discernment liberates us from societal pressures, internal expectations, and fleeting impulses. By practicing this rule, we empower ourselves to act with clarity, purpose, and integrity.

Living a Life of Intentional Choices

Rule #19 is a call to mindful action, urging us to focus on what truly serves our values and aspirations. By practicing discernment, we're choosing to live not by default but by design. This approach creates a life of depth and purpose, where our actions align with who we are and what we want to become. In the end, "just because you can, doesn't mean you should" is more than a reminder—it's a pathway to a more thoughtful, intentional, and fulfilling life. When we choose to act only on what aligns with our values and goals, we're not just making better decisions; we're creating a life that reflects our highest self.

Rule #20:
If you stay ready, you don't need to get ready

The Power of Preparedness

Preparation is more than a series of tasks; it's a mindset, a way of living that enables us to face opportunities and challenges with confidence. **Rule #20 "If You Stay Ready, You Don't Need to Get Ready"** reminds us that when we adopt a lifestyle of readiness, we're always poised to seize opportunities, adapt to change, and handle the unexpected. By staying ready, we minimize stress, enhance our agility, and create a foundation for sustained success. This rule explores how living with a state of readiness can benefit us in all aspects of life. From career advancement to personal growth, relationships, and health, staying ready empowers us to respond with intention, adapt swiftly, and move toward our goals with clarity and purpose.

Why Readiness Matters

In life, timing can make all the difference. Opportunities often arrive without warning, and challenges don't wait for us to be fully prepared. When we stay ready, we remove the need to scramble or rush into preparation, giving ourselves the advantage of a calm, collected response. Staying ready means keeping ourselves mentally, emotionally, and physically prepared to meet whatever comes our way. It's about consistent growth, regular reflection, and intentional habits that ensure we're always in a position to act, not react. This state of readiness reduces stress, fosters resilience, and builds confidence.

The Mindset of Readiness

Readiness isn't about living in constant vigilance or worry; it's about embracing consistency and discipline as tools for freedom. When we adopt a mindset of readiness, we approach life with curiosity, openness, and a commitment to self-improvement. We recognize that every small habit, every choice, and every bit of knowledge contributes to our ability to handle the future. The mindset of readiness is rooted in self-trust. By staying prepared, we trust ourselves to handle new situations, adapt to unexpected challenges, and embrace new opportunities without hesitation. This mindset reduces fear, enhances our resilience, and empowers us to take bold steps forward, knowing we're equipped to manage whatever comes.

Key Areas for Cultivating Readiness

Staying ready means maintaining a foundation of preparation in multiple areas of life so you're poised to meet opportunities and challenges head-on. Here are some essential areas where readiness can have a powerful impact:

- **Professional Development**: By continually honing your skills, staying informed about industry trends, and maintaining an updated resume or portfolio, you're ready to seize career opportunities when they arise. Professional readiness allows you to embrace promotions, tackle new projects, or pivot in your career with confidence.

- **Physical and Mental Health**: Health is the foundation of our energy and resilience. By maintaining a regular exercise routine, eating well, and managing stress, you build a baseline of wellness that enables you to stay strong and focused. Mental readiness is equally important; practicing mindfulness, stress management, and emotional resilience ensures you're prepared to handle life's highs and lows.

97

- **Financial Stability**: Financial readiness means having a plan, savings, and a budget that supports your goals and provides a safety net for the unexpected. By managing your finances proactively, you're better prepared to handle emergencies, seize investment opportunities, or pursue passions without constant financial stress.

- **Personal Relationships**: Relationships thrive when they're nurtured consistently. Staying ready in relationships means communicating openly, showing appreciation, and being there for others. By investing in relationships regularly, you're prepared to offer support or celebrate successes when the time comes, strengthening bonds and building a support network.

- **Personal Growth and Learning**: Lifelong learning keeps you adaptable, curious, and open to new experiences. Staying ready means consistently exploring new ideas, reading, taking courses, and developing new skills. This commitment to growth ensures that you're mentally agile and capable of embracing new challenges.

<u>Practical Strategies for Staying Ready</u>

1. **Establish Daily Habits of Growth:** Consistent habits build a foundation of readiness. Whether it's reading each day, exercising, or setting daily intentions, small, regular actions create lasting progress. These habits form the groundwork that enables you to face new opportunities with confidence.

2. **Stay Organized and Proactive:** Organization is key to readiness. Maintain a structured schedule, keep important documents updated, and plan ahead. Regularly reviewing and organizing your personal and professional life makes it easier to respond to new opportunities and challenges without feeling overwhelmed.

3. **Set Regular Checkpoints for Reflection:** Reflecting on your goals, values, and progress helps you stay aligned with your readiness goals. Set aside time to assess where you are, where you want to be, and whether you're taking the necessary steps to stay prepared. This keeps you on track and adaptable to changing circumstances.

4. **Anticipate and Plan for Potential Challenges:** Think through potential challenges or changes that could come your way. By planning in advance—whether it's building an emergency fund, honing a backup skill, or practicing stress management techniques—you're better equipped to handle difficulties calmly and effectively.

5. **Embrace Flexibility and Adaptability:** Staying ready doesn't mean rigidly sticking to plans; it means being adaptable. Embrace flexibility as a strength, recognizing that readiness is about responding thoughtfully to new information or situations. Flexibility keeps you agile and able to shift gears without losing momentum.

<u>The Freedom of a Ready Mindset</u>

When we stay ready, we gain a profound sense of freedom. We're not weighed down by the need to rush or the fear of missing out. Instead, we live with confidence, knowing that we're prepared to handle life's opportunities and challenges. This freedom allows us to embrace risks, take on new experiences, and explore possibilities without being held back by insecurity. A ready mindset empowers us to say "yes" when it matters and "no" when it doesn't align with our goals. It gives us the clarity to make intentional decisions and confident in our capacity to handle the consequences. This sense of freedom turns life's unexpected moments into opportunities rather than obstacles.

Practical Scenarios of Staying Ready in Action

- **Career Opportunities**: Imagine being approached for a job opportunity that aligns perfectly with your goals. Because you've kept your resume updated, maintained professional connections, and stayed informed about industry trends, you're able to act on this opportunity immediately, presenting yourself with confidence and readiness.

- **Health and Well-Being**: By maintaining regular exercise and stress management routines, you're better equipped to handle a physically demanding or stressful period. Your commitment to wellness provides the energy and resilience needed to navigate challenging times without burnout.

- **Financial Flexibility**: When an unexpected expense arises, or an exciting investment opportunity presents itself, your financial readiness—savings, a well-planned budget, and a safety net—allows you to respond without financial strain. You're able to seize opportunities without jeopardizing your stability.

Avoiding the Pitfalls of Over-Preparation

Staying ready doesn't mean obsessively planning for every possible outcome. Over-preparation can lead to anxiety, inflexibility, and missed opportunities. Remember, readiness is about creating a foundation, not controlling every variable. Balance preparation with openness to the unexpected, knowing that adaptability is a key part of readiness. The goal is to create a level of readiness that supports, rather than restricts, your ability to respond to life. Instead of preparing for every specific situation, focus on developing skills, habits, and a mindset that allows you to pivot and thrive, no matter what comes your way.

Living a Life of Empowered Readiness

Staying ready is about creating a life that reflects your goals, values, and aspirations. By preparing intentionally, building habits of resilience, and nurturing a flexible mindset, you're creating an environment where you can respond to life with confidence and purpose. This approach allows you to engage fully with each opportunity, knowing that you're equipped to handle both the rewards and the challenges. Embracing Rule #20 is more than a practice; it's a way of living that respects your potential, conserves your energy, and honors your growth. By staying ready, you're not only setting yourself up for success but also building a life that feels purposeful, empowered, and truly your own. When you live ready, you don't just react to life—you lead it.

Rule #21:
Cooperation over competition

The Strength of Collaboration

In a world often driven by rivalry, **Rule #21 "Cooperation Over Competition"** is a reminder of the power of working together. While competition has its place, cooperation opens doors to possibilities that individual effort alone cannot achieve. This rule is about embracing collaboration as a pathway to success, fulfillment, and personal growth. By prioritizing cooperation, we not only create stronger, more supportive connections but also cultivate an environment where everyone can thrive. This rule explores the benefits of cooperation over competition, how to build a collaborative mindset, and practical ways to foster teamwork in both personal and professional settings. Embracing cooperation enables us to build lasting relationships, strengthen communities, and work toward goals that serve more than just ourselves.

Why Cooperation Is More Powerful Than Competition

Competition often focuses on scarcity—the idea that there's only so much success, recognition, or happiness to go around. This mindset can foster jealousy, stress, and even conflict, as individuals feel they must outperform others to achieve their goals. Cooperation, however, shifts the focus from scarcity to abundance. By working together, we pool resources, share strengths, and support each other's growth, creating outcomes that benefit everyone involved. When we cooperate, we're not just pursuing personal goals; we're contributing to a larger purpose, a shared success that amplifies our collective strengths. Cooperation encourages open communication, mutual respect, and a sense of belonging, fostering a supportive environment where people feel empowered to share ideas, ask for help, and celebrate each other's achievements.

The Benefits of Choosing Cooperation Over Competition

Choosing cooperation over competition offers benefits that competition alone cannot match. A collaborative mindset fosters innovation and creativity by bringing diverse perspectives together, allowing fresh ideas and creative solutions to emerge in ways that a competitive environment often stifles. When people feel free to share their insights, they are more likely to experiment, take risks, and think outside the box. Cooperation also strengthens relationships and trust, as supporting each other's success builds bonds rooted in mutual respect and shared values, leading to deeper and more meaningful connections. Additionally, a cooperative approach encourages shared learning and growth, where knowledge, skills, and experiences are exchanged freely, creating an environment of continuous improvement. Unlike the stress and anxiety often associated with competition, cooperation fosters a sense of community and belonging, reducing stress and promoting well-being by ensuring that success is a shared effort. Finally, cooperation amplifies impact, allowing individuals to pool resources, skills, and energy to achieve results far greater than any one person could accomplish alone. Through shared victories, cooperation proves to be a powerful and enriching approach to achieving collective success.

Building a Cooperative Mindset

Shifting from a competitive mindset to a cooperative one requires a conscious effort to redefine success, let go of ego, and see others as allies rather than rivals. This shift begins with the understanding that someone else's success doesn't diminish our own. Instead, a cooperative mindset embraces the idea that by lifting others up, we elevate ourselves as well. Cultivating this mindset involves focusing on shared goals, where others are seen not as obstacles but as collaborators working toward common objectives. Practicing empathy and humility is key, as recognizing and respecting different perspectives fosters trust and connection. Celebrating collective success reinforces a culture of mutual support by acknowledging that the achievements of others contribute to the greater good. Finally, letting go of zero-sum thinking and adopting an abundance mindset helps us see that success is not a limited resource. When we embrace the belief that there's enough for everyone, we become more willing to share opportunities, ideas, and resources, strengthening the bonds that enable collective progress.

Practical Strategies for Embracing Cooperation

1. **Seek Win-Win Solutions:** In every interaction, look for ways to create mutual benefit. Whether it's negotiating a work project, solving a problem, or setting goals, focus on solutions that serve both parties. This approach encourages open dialogue and fosters positive outcomes that satisfy everyone involved.

2. **Encourage Open Communication:** Make an effort to communicate openly, sharing ideas, challenges, and feedback constructively. By creating an atmosphere where people feel safe to express themselves, you encourage collaboration and minimize misunderstandings. Open communication also allows you to address potential conflicts before they become obstacles.

3. **Build Inclusive Teams:** Bring together people with diverse skills, perspectives, and backgrounds. Inclusivity strengthens cooperation by ensuring that everyone has a voice and that a wide range of insights contribute to the outcome. When teams are inclusive, people feel valued, and they're more likely to contribute fully and authentically.

4. **Offer Help and Ask for Support:** Be proactive in offering your skills and resources to others, and don't hesitate to ask for help when you need it. This reciprocity creates a culture of support and fosters relationships based on trust. By offering assistance, you're reinforcing the idea that everyone's success matters.

5. **Focus on Process, Not Just Outcome:** Cooperation is often about the journey as much as the destination. Focus on creating a process that values teamwork, respect, and open communication. When people feel engaged and valued in the process, they're more invested in achieving the best possible outcome together.

<u>Overcoming Challenges in Cooperation</u>

Cooperation can present challenges, particularly in environments or relationships where competition is deeply ingrained. However, with patience, empathy, and commitment, these challenges can become opportunities for growth. One common hurdle is dealing with resistance, as not everyone may immediately embrace a collaborative approach. Some may believe competition is essential for motivation. In such cases, leading by example can be powerful—demonstrate the value of cooperation through your actions and highlight its positive outcomes. Another challenge is balancing individual and collective goals. Cooperation doesn't mean abandoning personal ambitions; instead, it's about finding ways to align your goals with those of the group, ensuring mutual success. Conflicts can also arise, but they don't have to derail collaboration. Address disagreements openly and constructively, focusing on solutions rather than assigning blame. By navigating conflicts with a cooperative mindset, you can build stronger relationships and find resolutions that honor everyone's perspectives. Through these approaches, challenges to cooperation can become stepping stones to deeper connections and shared success.

Real-Life Scenarios of Cooperation Over Competition

- **In the Workplace**: Imagine a team working on a challenging project. Instead of competing for recognition, team members share ideas freely, support each other's efforts, and celebrate small victories along the way. This cooperative approach creates a strong, unified team that's better equipped to tackle challenges and deliver outstanding results.

- **In Personal Relationships**: A cooperative mindset in relationships means prioritizing shared happiness and mutual respect over winning arguments or being right. Partners who focus on cooperation are more willing to compromise, listen to each other, and work toward solutions that enhance the relationship rather than focusing on individual gain.

- **In Personal Development**: Instead of comparing yourself to others, focus on cooperating with those who share similar goals. Join groups, share resources, and support each other's growth. This approach creates a positive environment where everyone's progress is celebrated, and personal growth becomes a shared journey.

The Legacy of a Cooperative Approach

Choosing cooperation over competition creates a legacy of connection, respect, and positive impact. By embracing this rule, we're contributing to an environment where people feel valued, supported, and motivated to reach their full potential. This legacy extends beyond individual interactions, influencing communities, workplaces, and relationships in profound ways. When we lead with cooperation, we inspire others to do the same. We create a ripple effect of kindness, empathy, and generosity, showing that success doesn't have to come at the expense of others. Instead, true success is about creating spaces where everyone can thrive, where each person's strengths are recognized, and where shared goals lead to shared victories.

Living a Life of Cooperation

Embracing Rule #21 is a choice to live with empathy, open-mindedness, and a commitment to the greater good. By prioritizing cooperation over competition, we're choosing a path that enriches not only our own lives but also the lives of those around us. We're building a world where success is collaborative, growth is shared, and fulfillment is found in uplifting one another. In the end, cooperation over competition isn't just a rule; it's a philosophy that creates stronger communities, deeper relationships, and a more fulfilling life. By working together, we're not just achieving goals; we're building a world where success is abundant, meaningful, and within reach for everyone.

Rule #22:
Challenge your assumptions, question everything

The Power of Curiosity and Critical Thinking

Our assumptions shape the way we view the world, interpret experiences, and make decisions. Yet, many of these assumptions go unexamined, limiting our understanding and potential. **Rule #22 "Challenge Your Assumptions, Question Everything"** encourages us to develop a mindset of curiosity and critical thinking, to look beyond surface-level beliefs, and to seek deeper truths continuously. By questioning our assumptions, we open ourselves to growth, adaptability, and greater clarity. This rule explores why challenging assumptions are essential for personal growth, how to cultivate a mindset that questions the status quo, and practical steps for transforming fixed beliefs into flexible insights. Embracing this rule enables us to approach life with an open mind, recognizing that there is always more to learn, understand, and discover.

Why Questioning Assumptions Matters

Assumptions can be helpful shortcuts, allowing us to make quick decisions and navigate familiar situations efficiently. However, they also create blind spots, leading to choices based on incomplete or outdated information. By questioning assumptions, we give ourselves the opportunity to make decisions that reflect current realities and align more closely with our goals and values. This process helps us overcome limiting beliefs that restrict our sense of possibility, opening the door to new opportunities and ways of thinking. It also enhances decision-making by encouraging us to gather accurate information and make better-informed choices. In relationships, questioning assumptions fosters empathy and clearer communication, reducing misunderstandings and building stronger connections. Additionally, it enables us to adapt to change, freeing us from outdated beliefs and keeping us open to new perspectives as the world evolves. Challenging assumptions isn't about discarding every belief but about evaluating and refining our understanding, ensuring our perspectives remain informed, balanced, and flexible.

The Mindset of Curiosity

To challenge our assumptions, we must cultivate a mindset of curiosity—one that embraces uncertainty and seeks to explore new ideas with openness and wonder. Curiosity encourages us to approach the world not just for answers but for the joy of learning and understanding. It involves striving to understand rather than judge, allowing us to engage with situations without labeling them as simply "right" or "wrong." It also means embracing ambiguity and recognizing that life is complex and not everything has a clear answer. A curious mindset helps us remain open to multiple possibilities. Additionally, curiosity transforms mistakes into valuable learning opportunities, encouraging us to question and refine our assumptions rather than fearing missteps. By cultivating curiosity, we approach life as eager learners, constantly expanding our understanding and improving our perspective.

Practical Strategies for Challenging Assumptions

1. **Ask, "Why?" Often:** Whenever you encounter a belief or assumption, ask yourself why you hold it. Dig deeper into the reasons behind your beliefs, and explore if they're based on evidence, experience, or simply tradition. This questioning process can reveal whether your assumptions are valid or in need of adjustment.

2. **Seek Multiple Perspectives:** Talk to people with different backgrounds, experiences, and viewpoints. Exposing yourself to diverse perspectives helps you see beyond your assumptions, offering a broader, more nuanced understanding. By engaging with different viewpoints, you gain insights that challenge your assumptions and enrich your knowledge.

3. **Challenge "Always" and "Never" Statements:** Statements that include words like "always" or "never" often signal rigid assumptions. When you catch yourself thinking or saying these words, pause and consider exceptions to these absolutes. Challenging these statements opens your mind to more flexible, realistic perspectives.

4. **Experiment with New Experiences:** Trying new activities, visiting new places, or learning new skills can shake up your routine assumptions and show you different ways of viewing the world. By stepping outside of your comfort zone, you break free from familiar patterns and create space for fresh insights and discoveries.

5. **Practice Reflective Journaling:** Use journaling as a tool to explore your thoughts, beliefs, and assumptions. Reflect on recent experiences and question why you reacted or thought the way you did. Journaling allows you to dig deeper into your beliefs and discover assumptions that may be influencing your decisions subconsciously.

<u>Recognizing and Overcoming Cognitive Biases</u>

Our assumptions are often influenced by cognitive biases—mental shortcuts that shape our perception and interpretation of information. By learning to recognize and question these biases, we become better equipped to make objective, informed choices.

Common biases include:

- **Confirmation Bias**: The tendency to favor information that supports our existing beliefs. To counter this, intentionally seek out information that challenges your views.

- **Availability Bias**: The tendency to rely on immediate examples or recent information. Be mindful of this bias by gathering a broader range of information and not relying solely on what's readily accessible.

- **Anchoring Bias**: The tendency to rely heavily on the first piece of information encountered. Practice revisiting initial assumptions and gathering additional data before concluding.

Recognizing these biases is the first step in challenging them. By doing so, you become more conscious of how your assumptions are formed and gain the ability to view situations more objectively.

The Importance of Flexibility in Beliefs

Challenging assumptions requires cultivating flexibility in your beliefs. When we hold onto beliefs too rigidly, we risk closing ourselves off to new information and opportunities. Flexibility doesn't mean abandoning your values; rather, it's about being willing to adapt your understanding as you gain new insights. Flexible beliefs enable us to adapt to new information, recognizing that life and knowledge are constantly evolving. This adaptability allows us to update our assumptions based on fresh evidence and experiences. Flexibility also fosters personal growth by encouraging us to remain open to change, learning, and evolution rather than being stifled by rigid thinking. Additionally, it reduces conflict by lowering defensiveness in conversations, creating space for respectful and constructive dialogue. By embracing flexibility, we hold our beliefs thoughtfully, ready to evolve when new insights arise, rather than clinging to assumptions out of habit or fear.

Real-Life Scenarios of Challenging Assumptions

- **In Relationships**: You may assume you know why a friend or partner is behaving a certain way based on past experiences. Instead, ask them about their feelings and motivations. Challenging assumptions in relationships promotes understanding and prevents misunderstandings rooted in unspoken expectations.

- **In the Workplace**: Assume you're preparing for a project and have ideas based on past successes. Rather than relying solely on old methods, challenge your assumptions by asking, "Is this the best approach for this unique situation?" This flexibility can lead to innovation and improved results.

- **In Personal Goals**: Perhaps you believe that success means following a specific career path or achieving certain milestones. Questioning this assumption may reveal that true success, for you, is about fulfillment, creativity, or impact— insights that could open new, more aligned possibilities.

Embracing Growth Through Curiosity

By challenging assumptions and questioning everything, we become lifelong learners, open to the richness and diversity of human experience. This approach promotes growth, adaptability, and a sense of wonder that keeps us engaged with the world. Growth through curiosity isn't just about finding answers; it's about exploring possibilities, expanding our perspectives, and discovering paths that align with our truest selves. When we adopt a mindset that questions everything, we're not seeking to be contrary but to be conscious. We're committing to a life of thoughtful inquiry, one that enriches our understanding and leads to decisions rooted in awareness and intention.

Living a Life of Open-Minded Inquiry

Rule #22 encourages us to approach life with a spirit of inquiry and a willingness to question the familiar. This open-minded inquiry not only deepens our understanding but also enriches our relationships, sharpens our decision-making, and frees us from limiting beliefs. By challenging assumptions, we gain the ability to see the world more clearly, make choices that align with our values, and approach life with a sense of exploration and possibility. In the end, "Challenge Your Assumptions, Question Everything" is a pathway to a life of authenticity, wisdom, and endless discovery. When we question everything, we're choosing to live with curiosity, courage, and the excitement of constant growth.

Rule #23:
Never lie to yourself

The Power of Self-Honesty

At the heart of personal growth and fulfillment lies a foundational principle: self-honesty. **Rule #23 "Never Lie to Yourself"** is about developing a deep commitment to knowing and accepting the truth about who we are, what we want, and what we're capable of. Self-deception may offer short-term comfort, but it comes at the expense of clarity, progress, and inner peace. By choosing to face ourselves honestly, we gain the power to make authentic choices, grow, and ultimately create a life that reflects our truest self. This rule explores why self-honesty is essential for genuine growth, the ways in which self-deception can manifest, and practical strategies for cultivating honesty with yourself. By committing to truth, we empower ourselves to overcome obstacles, pursue goals with clarity, and live a life that feels deeply meaningful and aligned.

Why Self-Honesty Is Essential

Self-honesty is the cornerstone of self-respect, resilience, and authenticity. By being honest with ourselves, we gain a clear understanding of our strengths, weaknesses, desires, and fears. This clarity allows us to make choices that support personal growth and align with our values. In contrast, self-deception creates a disconnect between our inner truth and the lives we build, leading to internal conflict and dissatisfaction. Self-honesty empowers us to make authentic choices that reflect our true desires rather than conforming to societal expectations or what we think we "should" want. It helps us overcome limiting patterns by recognizing and breaking free from behaviors and beliefs that no longer serve us. This honesty fosters inner peace by harmonizing our inner world with our outer actions and builds resilience by preparing us to face challenges with purpose and strength. By prioritizing self-honesty, we choose to live consciously and purposefully, crafting a life that feels genuine and fulfilling.

Recognizing Self-Deception

Self-deception often operates subtly, masking itself as rationalization, denial, or avoidance, making it easy to overlook its presence in our lives. These deceptions can limit our growth, obscure our potential, and prevent us from making choices that genuinely serve our well-being and goals. Recognizing self-deception requires self-awareness and a willingness to confront ourselves without judgment or defensiveness. Common forms of self-deception include rationalizing unhealthy habits and convincing ourselves that certain indulgences or behaviors are justified even when they harm our well-being. It also involves dismissing red flags in relationships, work, or health by downplaying warning signs and hoping they will resolve themselves. Another form is underestimating our potential, convincing ourselves we're not capable or ready for something, and avoiding risks that could lead to growth. Lastly, self-deception manifests as overlooking personal responsibility blaming external factors instead of acknowledging our role in challenges or setbacks. By becoming aware of these patterns, we can address self-deception directly, empowering ourselves to make choices rooted in truth rather than avoidance.

Practical Strategies for Cultivating Self-Honesty

1. **Practice Regular Self-Reflection:** Take time to reflect on your thoughts, actions, and emotions. Journaling or meditating can help you explore your inner world and identify areas where you may be avoiding the truth. Regular self-reflection fosters self-awareness, creating space to confront and understand your true motivations.

2. **Ask Yourself the Hard Questions:** Honest self-inquiry involves asking questions that reveal deeper truths. Questions like "What am I avoiding?" "What do I really want?" or "Am I living in alignment with my values?" can shed light on areas of self-deception. Answering honestly, without judgment, allows you to see yourself more clearly.

3. **Embrace Self-Compassion:** Self-honesty can sometimes reveal uncomfortable truths, but it's important to approach yourself with compassion. Avoid harsh self-criticism; instead, acknowledge your flaws and mistakes with kindness. Self-compassion fosters growth, making it easier to accept and work through difficult truths.

4. **Seek Feedback from Trusted Sources:** Sometimes, those who know us well can see things we might overlook. Seek feedback from people you trust and respect, asking for their honest perspective. Listening to outside views with an open mind can reveal blind spots, helping you see yourself more objectively.

5. **Commit to Small Acts of Truthfulness:** Self-honesty is a practice that grows over time. Start with small acts of truthfulness—acknowledge when you're procrastinating, admit when you're avoiding something difficult, or recognize when you're not acting in alignment with your goals. These small acts build the habit of honesty, making it easier to be truthful in bigger areas of life.

The Cost of Self-Deception

Self-deception may provide temporary comfort, but it comes with a significant cost. When we ignore or distort the truth, we limit our potential and hinder our progress. Self-deception can lead to unfulfilling careers, strained relationships, and even health issues if we continually avoid facing the truth about our choices and their consequences. Over time, self-deception creates a disconnect between who we are and who we want to be. This dissonance leads to feelings

116

of dissatisfaction, frustration, and even resentment. By embracing self-honesty, we close this gap, aligning our actions with our values and building a life that reflects our authentic selves.

Living with Integrity

Integrity begins with self-honesty. When we're truthful with ourselves, we're able to live with integrity, aligning our beliefs, actions, and words. This alignment builds self-respect, as we know we're acting in ways that reflect our core values. Living with integrity also creates trust with others, as people sense and appreciate our authenticity. Integrity is not about perfection; it's about consistency. When we commit to self-honesty, we're committing to show up authentically, even when it's difficult. This integrity strengthens our character, reinforcing our commitment to a life that's meaningful, purposeful, and true to who we are.

Real-Life Scenarios of Practicing Self-Honesty

- **Career Choices**: Suppose you're in a job that no longer fulfills you, yet you tell yourself you "have to stay" because it's safe or familiar. By acknowledging your dissatisfaction honestly, you open the door to exploring other opportunities that align with your passions and strengths, creating a more fulfilling career path.

- **Personal Relationships**: Perhaps you're in a friendship or relationship that has become unhealthy, but you convince yourself that it's "not that bad." Practicing self-honesty allows you to confront your true feelings, empowering you to set boundaries or move on if necessary, creating space for relationships that truly support your well-being.

- **Health and Well-Being**: Let's say you've been neglecting your health, telling yourself that you'll "get to it later." By facing the truth about the impact of these choices, you're more likely to take action, building habits that support your long-term health and vitality.

Embracing Self-Acceptance Through Honesty

Self-honesty isn't about judging ourselves or dwelling on our flaws; it's about accepting who we are with compassion and clarity. When we face ourselves honestly, we're able to make peace with our imperfections, viewing them as opportunities for growth rather than sources of shame. This self-acceptance liberates us from the need to hide or pretend, allowing us to show up fully and authentically. By embracing self-acceptance, we're free to pursue our goals without fear of failure or judgment. We become empowered to take risks, make changes, and move forward in ways that honor our true selves.

Living a Life Rooted in Truth

Living by Rule #23 is about committing to a life rooted in truth, both with ourselves and others. It's about making the courageous choice to face ourselves, even when it's uncomfortable, and using that truth to guide our decisions, relationships, and growth. When we stop lying to ourselves, we gain clarity, resilience, and a deep sense of purpose. By choosing self-honesty, we create a foundation of authenticity that enriches every area of life. We move through the world with a clear sense of who we are, what we want, and what we're capable of achieving. In the end, Rule #23 isn't just a guideline; it's a pathway to living a life that's real, rewarding, and true to who we are at our core. Embracing self-honesty is a courageous act, one that empowers us to live fully and unapologetically. It's a commitment to ourselves, a promise to show up with integrity, and a testament to the value of truth in creating a life that feels deeply fulfilling and aligned.

Rule #24:
Practice your passions

Passions are the driving forces that bring vibrancy, joy, and purpose into our lives. **Rule #24 "Practice Your Passions"** is a reminder to make time for the things that truly ignite our souls. In the hustle of daily life, it's easy to relegate our passions to the sidelines, treating them as luxuries rather than priorities. Yet, practicing our passions is essential for personal growth, creativity, and fulfillment. By cultivating our passions, we nurture a deeper sense of self and create a life filled with purpose and joy. This rule explores why it's crucial to invest time in our passions, how to overcome the obstacles that often stand in the way, and practical strategies for integrating our passions into daily life. Embracing our passions isn't just about enhancing our own lives; it's about contributing to the world with the unique energy and creativity that only we can bring.

Why Practicing Your Passions Matters

Our passions reflect our deepest interests and desires, often making us feel most alive, inspired, and engaged. Practicing our passions connects us with our authentic selves, allowing us to embrace our natural talents and explore the aspects of life that genuinely excite us. Passion fuels creativity, motivates growth, and provides an outlet for expression that is both fulfilling and enriching. Engaging with our passions fosters personal growth by challenging us to learn, evolve, and refine our skills. It enhances well-being by offering an escape from stress and bringing joy and a sense of accomplishment. As we improve in areas we love, our confidence grows, empowering us to take risks and pursue new challenges.

Passion also creates a sense of purpose, providing direction and meaning to our lives and helping us feel aligned with our true selves. Additionally, sharing our passions inspires others, builds connections, and contributes to communities of shared interests and values. By prioritizing our passions, we nurture happiness, self-fulfillment, and a deeper sense of purpose that enhances every area of our lives.

Overcoming Obstacles to Practicing Your Passions

Life's demands often make it difficult to focus on our passions. Responsibilities, time constraints, self-doubt, and societal expectations can all discourage us from pursuing the things that bring us joy. However, by recognizing these obstacles and finding ways to overcome them, we can create space for our passions, no matter how busy life becomes. Time constraints often feel overwhelming, but even dedicating a few minutes each day to your passion can make a meaningful difference. Fear of imperfection may hold us back, yet it's important to remember that practicing our passions is about enjoyment, not achieving perfection. Self-doubt can also deter us, but passion grows with practice, and each small step builds confidence over time. Additionally, many people feel guilty about prioritizing their passions, viewing them as selfish, but nurturing what we love benefits not only ourselves but also those around us by making us happier and more fulfilled. By acknowledging these challenges, we can address them head-on and treat our passions as valuable and integral parts of our lives rather than optional indulgences.

Practical Strategies for Practicing Your Passions

1. **Dedicate Consistent Time, No Matter How Small:** Set aside a specific time each day, week, or month to work on your passion, even if it's only 10 minutes. Consistency is key to making progress, and a small amount of time dedicated regularly can have a big impact over time.

2. **Create a Passion-Friendly Environment:** Designate a space in your home or workspace for practicing your passion. Whether it's a corner for painting, a desk for writing, or a quiet spot for meditation, having a designated space reminds you to engage with your passion regularly.

3. **Set Small, Achievable Goals:** Break down your passion into manageable steps or projects. Setting small, achievable goals helps build momentum and provides a sense of accomplishment, encouraging you to continue. For instance, if your passion is photography, set a goal to capture one meaningful photo each day.

4. **Connect with Like-Minded People:** Joining groups or communities of people who share your passion can provide motivation, inspiration, and accountability. Surrounding yourself with others who value and practice similar passions can keep you inspired and help you stay committed.

5. **Embrace Imperfection and Enjoy the Process:** Remember that passion is about the joy of the process, not achieving perfection. Allow yourself to experiment, make mistakes, and explore freely. Embracing imperfection liberates you to create without pressure, helping you stay engaged and enthusiastic.

How Practicing Passions Enhances Other Areas of Life

Practicing our passions creates a ripple effect, positively influencing all areas of life. Engaging in activities we love rejuvenates us, making us more resilient and effective in work, relationships, and personal development. By prioritizing our passions, we fuel our happiness and sense of fulfillment, which in turn strengthens our energy and enthusiasm for everything we do. Pursuing passions reduces stress by offering a reprieve from daily pressures improving focus, productivity, and mental well-being. It also fuels creativity, bringing fresh ideas and perspectives to our work and other aspects of life. Engaging in what we love helps us bring a happier, more fulfilled version of ourselves to our relationships, enriching our connections with others.

Additionally, taking breaks to pursue passions enhances productivity, recharging our mental and emotional energy to improve focus and efficiency. Above all, practicing passions reinforces a sense of personal fulfillment, providing purpose and joy that elevate our quality of life. Incorporating passions into our routines allows us to approach life with renewed resilience, enthusiasm, and purpose that resonates throughout everything we do.

Real-Life Scenarios of Practicing Your Passions

- **The Busy Professional**: Suppose you have a demanding job but love playing the guitar. By dedicating just 10 minutes each evening to practicing a favorite song, you're reconnecting with something that brings joy, helping you unwind and providing a creative outlet that balances work stress.

- **The Parent with Limited Free Time**: If you're a parent who loves painting, you might feel there's no time for your passion. However, setting aside 30 minutes on weekends to create small sketches or paintings can keep your passion alive, offering a sense of personal accomplishment and joy.

- **The Student Exploring Identity**: As a student passionate about creative writing, dedicating time each week to write short stories or poems helps you express yourself and develop your voice. This practice can also enhance self-confidence and create a meaningful way to explore your identity.

Making Passion a Lifelong Practice

Embracing our passions is not a one-time effort but a lifelong practice that evolves as we grow and change. Our passions may take new forms or lead us in unexpected directions, requiring flexibility, curiosity, and a commitment to nurturing what brings us joy. By treating passions as an ongoing practice, we commit to living with authenticity, vitality, and a continuous sense of discovery. Making passion a lifelong practice means staying open to new interests, being willing to explore fresh pursuits as they emerge, and allowing them to keep our lives vibrant. It also involves prioritizing what we love by regularly reevaluating our schedules and commitments to ensure we make time for our passions, even as they grow or shift. Embracing growth and learning is equally important, as passion is a journey of refinement and exploration. Each practice session becomes an opportunity to learn, try new techniques, and develop our skills over time. By committing to this lifelong practice, we ensure that our lives remain rich, purposeful, and deeply connected to what inspires us.

Living a Life Enriched by Passion

Practicing our passions is one of the most fulfilling ways to connect with our authentic selves, bringing joy, creativity, and purpose into our lives. Rule #24 is a call to prioritize what makes us feel alive, to embrace the activities and interests that bring us joy, and to make time for what truly matters to us. By committing to practice our passions, we're choosing to live a life that's vibrant, intentional, and filled with meaning. When we live a life enriched by passion, we're more than just productive; we're fulfilled. We create a world where joy, creativity, and purpose are not luxuries but essential parts of who we are. Practicing our passions is a gift we give to ourselves, and in doing so, we inspire others to do the same.

Rule #25:
Ask for what you want. The worst thing they can say is no

The Power of Asking

Many of us hold back from asking for what we want, afraid of rejection, disappointment, or the possibility of being told "no." **But Rule #25 "Ask for What You Want, The Worst Thing They Can Say Is No"** reminds us that the simple act of asking opens doors to opportunities, relationships, and experiences we might otherwise miss. By choosing to ask, we take an active role in creating our lives rather than passively waiting for things to fall into place. This rule explores the courage it takes to ask for what we want, the benefits of facing rejection, and practical strategies for making requests confidently and constructively. Embracing the power of asking empowers us to take ownership of our lives and brings us closer to the things we truly desire.

Why Asking Is Essential

Asking for what we want requires vulnerability, courage, and self-belief. It is a direct way to communicate our needs, ambitions, and desires, signaling to others—and ourselves—that our goals matter, our needs are valid, and we are worthy of what we seek. Whether it's a career opportunity, a personal relationship, or a life experience, asking is often the crucial first step toward achieving our goals. This practice builds confidence by reinforcing our sense of self-worth each time we ask while also creating opportunities that might not otherwise arise. Asking encourages authenticity, as it is a form of honest communication that allows us to express ourselves fully and without pretense. It also strengthens relationships by fostering trust and showing that we value the input and support of others. Even facing rejection teaches resilience, helping us handle "no" without internalizing it as a measure of our worth. When we embrace the habit of asking for what we want, we empower ourselves to shape our lives actively, creating a world where our dreams, needs, and ambitions are recognized and pursued.

Overcoming the Fear of "No"

Fear of rejection is one of the most common reasons people hesitate to ask for what they want. We often worry that a "no" will feel like a personal failure or erode our confidence. However, hearing "no" is often a necessary step on the journey toward achieving our goals. Each rejection is an opportunity to learn, adapt, and grow. By reframing rejection, we can view it as a redirection, where a "no" points us toward better opportunities or alternative paths we might not have considered. It also becomes a chance for reflection, encouraging us to reassess our approach, clarify our goals, or explore new ways of presenting our requests. Over time, rejection serves as a tool for resilience, making each "no" less intimidating and strengthening our determination to keep moving forward. When we learn to separate rejection from our self-worth, we see each "no" as a valuable part of the process, building our strength and bringing us closer to success.

Practical Strategies for Asking Confidently

1. **Be Clear and Specific:** Know exactly what you're asking for and communicate it clearly. Instead of vague or indirect hints, state your request in specific terms. Whether it's a promotion, a favor, or feedback, clarity shows confidence and ensures the other person understands what you're seeking.

2. **Believe in the Value of Your Request:** Before asking, take a moment to recognize the value of your request. Remind yourself why it's important to you and how it aligns with your goals or needs. Believing in the validity of your request strengthens your confidence and makes it easier for others to see its merit.

3. **Practice Mindful Timing:** Timing can greatly impact the outcome of a request. Consider the other person's schedule, priorities, and state of mind before making your ask. A well-timed request is more likely to be received positively, as it demonstrates respect for the other person's time and energy.

4. **Stay Open to Alternatives:** Sometimes, the exact thing we ask for may not be feasible, but an alternative solution might be. If someone isn't able to meet your request fully, consider other ways they might be able to help. Being open to alternatives shows flexibility and keeps the conversation positive.

5. **Accept "No" Gracefully:** When faced with rejection, respond with gratitude and grace. Thank the person for their time and consideration, and let them know you appreciate their honesty. Handling "no" with composure not only maintains the relationship but also strengthens your resilience and prepares you for future requests.

The Benefits of Asking in Different Areas of Life

The courage to ask for what we want can transform every aspect of our lives, from careers to personal relationships and personal growth. By practicing the art of asking, we break free from self-imposed limitations and create a life that aligns with our true desires. In careers and professional growth, asking for a raise, promotion, or more challenging responsibilities demonstrates initiative and self-confidence, signaling to employers that we value our contributions and are committed to growth. In relationships, asking for support, quality time, or open communication fosters healthier, more trusting connections based on mutual respect and honesty. For personal development, seeking feedback or mentorship provides valuable insights, highlighting areas for improvement and helping us refine our skills. Even in daily life, asking for assistance with tasks or favors reinforces the importance of community and shared responsibility, reminding us that we don't have to face challenges alone. Across all these areas, asking sends a powerful message that our needs and goals are worth pursuing. Each ask brings us closer to a life that feels authentic, fulfilling, and aligned with our true selves.

Real-Life Scenarios of Asking for What You Want

- **Career Advancement**: Suppose you've been working diligently and are ready for more responsibility. Instead of waiting for recognition, schedule a meeting with your manager, explain the value you've added, and express your interest in a promotion. Even if the answer is "not yet," you'll have initiated an important conversation, making your ambitions clear.

- **Strengthening Relationships**: If you're feeling the need for more support from a friend or partner, express it openly. Saying, "I would really appreciate it if we could spend some time together this weekend," lets them know how they can support you. This openness fosters understanding and connection.

- **Personal Growth**: If you're looking to improve a skill or gain insights, ask a mentor or trusted colleague for feedback. For example, "Could you provide feedback on my presentation skills? I'm looking to improve and value your perspective." Constructive feedback from others is invaluable for growth and self-awareness.

Embracing the Freedom of Asking

Learning to ask for what you want brings a sense of freedom and empowerment. By permitting yourself to ask, you're freeing yourself from unnecessary limits, fear, or hesitation. This freedom comes from the knowledge that asking is an act of courage and that each ask, regardless of the outcome, strengthens your resilience and builds confidence. Asking is not about entitlement; it's about taking responsibility for creating the life you envision. When we stop waiting for things to come to us and start actively asking, we're taking control of our path, moving forward with clarity and purpose. This freedom allows us to embrace our potential and pursue a life that reflects our true desires.

Living a Life of Empowered Asking

Rule #25 encourages us to let go of fear, to view "no" as simply part of the journey, and to embrace the power of asking as a path to a richer, more fulfilling life. When we make asking a habit, we're choosing to create opportunities, build connections, and assert our worth in every area of life. By asking for what we want, we're not just increasing our chances of success; we're affirming that our goals, needs, and dreams are valid and worth pursuing. In the end, asking is an act of self-respect, a way of showing ourselves and others that we believe in our potential and are committed to living authentically. Living a life of empowered asking means embracing the courage to face rejection, to take risks, and to trust that each "no" brings us closer to the "yes" we're waiting for. When we ask for what we want, we're choosing to live boldly, embracing the possibilities of a life fully lived and wholeheartedly pursued.

Rule #26:
Fall in love often

Love has the power to bring magic, meaning, and inspiration into our lives, yet too often, we reserve it only for relationships. **Rule #26 "Fall in Love Often, Particularly with Ideas, Art, Music, Literature, Food, and Far-Off Places"** invites us to expand our capacity for love beyond people and to find joy and wonder in the beauty that surrounds us every day. By choosing to fall in love with life itself, we open ourselves to the richness of experiences, creativity, and discovery, cultivating a sense of awe and gratitude for the world around us. This rule explores the transformative power of falling in love with life's many facets, how it nurtures our spirit and creativity, and practical ways to embrace this mindset. Falling in love often isn't just about experiencing joy—it's about nurturing curiosity, feeding the soul, and building a life that's full of wonder and possibility.

Why Falling in Love with Life Matters

When we allow ourselves to fall in love with new ideas, art, music, literature, food, and distant places, we enrich our inner worlds and create a deeper connection to the life around us. Each new fascination expands our perspective, teaches us something new, and can even ignite a hidden passion. Falling in love with life in all its forms fills us with enthusiasm and gratitude, making every day feel more meaningful. This mindset matters because it expands our minds, inviting us to embrace different ways of thinking and seeing the world. It fuels creativity and inspiration, captivating us with beauty and novelty that drives us to explore, imagine, and create. By engaging with diverse forms of art, cultures, and experiences, we deepen our appreciation for the unique and beautiful differences that make the world so rich. Falling in love with life also cultivates joy and fulfillment, helping us find meaning beyond material achievements and discover satisfaction in everyday moments. Moreover, it builds resilience by providing sources of joy and comfort during difficult times, reminding us of life's beauty and possibilities. Falling in love with life isn't about seeking entertainment—it's about engaging deeply with the world and discovering what truly makes us feel alive.

Falling in Love with People

Allowing yourself to fall in love with people is one of the most profound ways to experience connection, vulnerability, and growth. When we open our hearts to others, we embrace their uniqueness and allow their perspectives, energy, and presence to enrich our lives. Falling in love—whether romantically, platonically, or through deep admiration—teaches us empathy, patience, and the beauty of shared experiences. It reminds us of the value of human connection, encouraging us to trust, care, and invest in relationships that bring meaning and joy. While it involves vulnerability and the risk of heartache, the rewards of love far outweigh the fears. Love helps us see ourselves more clearly, fosters resilience, and brings a sense of belonging that is essential to a fulfilling life. By allowing ourselves to fall in love with people, we deepen our understanding of humanity and create bonds that give life its richest and most lasting meaning.

Falling in Love with Ideas

Ideas have the power to transform our thinking, challenge our beliefs, and inspire growth. When we fall in love with ideas, we cultivate a mindset of curiosity and openness, embracing new perspectives, philosophies, and innovations. Engaging with diverse viewpoints allows us to foster empathy and personal growth, whether through reading, conversation, or study. Following our curiosity deepens this connection, encouraging us to explore concepts or theories that excite us through research, learning, or discussion. Conversations with others can also be a gateway to fresh ideas, introducing us to unique insights that spark fascination and a desire to know more. Falling in love with ideas helps us become lifelong learners, continuously enriching our minds and deepening our understanding of the world around us.

Falling in Love with Art and Music

Art and music have the unique ability to evoke emotion, beauty, and expression in ways that transcend language and logic. When we fall in love with art and music, we open ourselves to profound sensory experiences, allowing them to move us and connect us to something greater. Visiting museums and attending concerts offers an opportunity to engage deeply, with each piece or performance serving as an invitation to feel, reflect, and imagine. Creating your own art, whether through painting, playing an instrument, or writing, provides a personal connection to the creative process and a deeper appreciation for artistic expression. Exploring different genres expands our horizons, introducing us to unfamiliar styles, artists, or songs that may ignite new inspiration. Falling in love with art and music nurtures our emotional depth, offering a powerful way to connect with ourselves and others in ways that words alone cannot express.

Falling in Love with Literature and Stories

Literature and stories are portals to different lives, eras, and worlds. When we fall in love with books and stories, we connect with characters, ideas, and emotions that shape us and provide new insights into our own lives. Reading widely exploring diverse genres, authors, and cultures, enriches our understanding and introduces us to stories that broaden our worldview. Joining a book club enhances this experience by sharing perspectives and discovering different interpretations of the same story. Reflecting on your reading, whether through journaling or discussion, deepens the impact by allowing you to explore themes, characters, and ideas on a personal level. Falling in love with literature nurtures empathy, imagination, and self-reflection, enabling us to journey beyond our own experiences into countless others.

Falling in Love with Food and Culinary Experiences

Food connects us to culture, history, and sensory pleasure, celebrating flavor, tradition, and creativity. Falling in love with food means embracing the joy it brings and the stories it tells. Exploring new cuisines, whether by visiting local restaurants, experimenting with recipes, or trying unfamiliar dishes, opens our taste buds and minds to different cultures and ways of life. Learning about food cultures adds depth to this experience, revealing the history and traditions behind certain dishes and highlighting food as a reflection of community and heritage. Cooking and sharing meals creates a hands-on connection to food, while the act of sharing enhances joy and fosters meaningful connections. Falling in love with food enriches our appreciation for culture, creativity, and the simple pleasure of a well-made meal, turning everyday moments into celebrations of life's richness.

Falling in Love with Far-off Places

Travel offers the opportunity to immerse ourselves in new cultures, landscapes, and ways of life. Falling in love with far-off places means embracing a spirit of exploration, seeing the world through fresh eyes, and allowing each destination to shape us in unique ways. Traveling with an open mind is key, approaching each journey with curiosity and respect, ready to learn from the people and places we encounter. This broadens our understanding and fosters compassion. Immersing yourself in local culture—by meeting people, exploring markets, and participating in traditions—creates a deeper and more meaningful travel experience than simply sightseeing. Even when traveling far isn't possible, adopting the mindset of a lifelong traveler keeps the spirit of exploration alive. By exploring new neighborhoods, trying unfamiliar activities, and finding beauty in your surroundings, you can carry the joy of discovery wherever you go. Falling in love with far-off places inspires wonder, humility, and a deep appreciation for the world's diversity and richness.

<u>Practical Tips for Falling in Love with Life</u>

1. **Make Space for Exploration:** Dedicate time each week to explore something new. Whether it's reading a book, trying a new cuisine, or visiting a local gallery, make room in your schedule for discovery.

2. **Embrace Childlike Curiosity:** Approach life with a sense of wonder and openness, as if seeing everything for the first time. Allow yourself to be fascinated, to ask questions, and to marvel at the world around you.

3. **Savor the Small Moments:** Falling in love with life doesn't always require grand gestures. Find beauty in small, everyday moments—a sunset, a favorite song, a cozy meal. Practicing gratitude for these experiences enhances your appreciation for life's simple joys.

4. **Stay Open to Change and Growth:** Allow yourself to evolve. What you fall in love with today may be different from tomorrow, and that's part of the journey. Embrace the fluidity of your passions, letting them shape and enrich your life as you grow.

5. **Share Your Enthusiasms:** Talk about what you love with others. Sharing your passions creates connections, deepens experiences, and inspires those around you to explore and discover as well.

Living a Life of Constant Discovery

By choosing to fall in love often, we're choosing to live fully and joyfully, open to the beauty and complexity of life. Each new fascination—whether it's an idea, a person, a work of art, a book, a dish, or a distant place—adds depth to our lives, filling our days with meaning, curiosity, and gratitude. Falling in love with life is about more than happiness; it's about nurturing a sense of wonder, a drive to explore, and a commitment to never stop learning. This mindset turns the world into a vast, ever-inspiring playground where each day is an opportunity to find something beautiful and new. In the end, Rule #26 encourages us to live with an open heart.

Rule #27:
Say what you mean and mean what you say

The Power of Authentic Communication

Clear, honest communication is one of the most important skills we can cultivate in life. **Rule #27 "Say What You Mean and Mean What You Say"** is about aligning our words with our intentions and values, building a foundation of trust, authenticity, and respect in our relationships. When we speak with clarity and honesty, we create connections that are genuine and meaningful, and we foster a life that reflects who we truly are. This rule explores why it's essential to speak authentically, how to practice saying what we mean, and the positive impact that honest communication has on ourselves and those around us. By saying what we mean and meaning what we say, we create a life rooted in integrity, strengthening our self-respect and the trust others place in us.

Why Authentic Communication Matters

Our words hold immense power—they can build trust, convey emotions, and express our needs. Speaking honestly fosters clarity and openness, allowing others to understand and connect with us on a deeper level. Conversely, when our words fail to align with our true feelings or intentions, we create confusion and mistrust. Authentic communication is not just about truthfulness; it's about choosing words that reflect our values, intentions, and beliefs, shaping a life that aligns with who we truly are. Authentic communication builds trust by demonstrating honesty, consistency, and dependability, ensuring others can rely on us. It creates clarity by preventing misunderstandings and allowing others to understand our intentions and needs fully. This type of communication strengthens relationships, fostering respect and connection that lead to deeper, more meaningful bonds. Speaking truthfully also enhances self-respect, as it honors our values and integrity, reinforcing a strong sense of self-worth. Furthermore, authenticity promotes personal growth by encouraging us to take responsibility for our actions and align our lives with our true selves. Committing to say what we mean and mean what we say is a commitment to integrity, clarity, and respect—for ourselves and for those we engage with.

The Importance of Aligning Words with Intentions

Saying what we mean requires self-awareness and a commitment to aligning our words with our intentions. It involves reflecting on what we truly think, feel, and need rather than defaulting to what is easiest or most socially acceptable. When our words align with our intentions, we communicate authentically, bringing our true selves into each interaction. This begins with knowing our true feelings by taking a moment to check in with ourselves before speaking. Understanding what we genuinely want to communicate helps ensure our message is clear and meaningful. Avoiding excessive politeness or sugar-coating is also essential; while respect is important, diluting our message with vague or overly polite language can obscure our true thoughts. Staying true to our values, even when it's uncomfortable, ensures that our communication reflects integrity and authenticity. Honesty in communication is more than simply telling the truth—it's about expressing ourselves openly, setting boundaries, and speaking up about our needs and feelings. This kind of honesty fosters trust and respect, both in our relationships and within ourselves, creating a foundation of authenticity that empowers us to live and connect more meaningfully.

Practicing Honesty in Communication

1. **Be Direct and Respectful:** Communicate your message clearly, using direct language that's easy to understand. Avoid vague or indirect language, and aim to be as concise as possible. At the same time, use a respectful tone that acknowledges the feelings of others, even when discussing challenging topics.

2. **Use "I" Statements:** Using "I" statements helps you express your feelings without blaming others. For example, say, "I feel overwhelmed when there's a lot to do," rather than, "You always give me too much work." "I" statements foster open dialogue and reduce defensiveness, allowing for more constructive conversations.

3. **Pause Before Speaking:** Take a moment to think before you speak, especially in emotional situations. Pausing allows you to clarify your thoughts and ensure that what you're about to say reflects your true intentions. This simple habit can prevent misunderstandings and reduce impulsive remarks.

4. **Be Willing to Say No:** Saying no is an essential part of honest communication. When we agree to things we don't want to do, we're not being true to ourselves. Saying no respectfully allows you to set boundaries and communicate your needs authentically.

5. **Acknowledge When You Don't Have an Answer:** If you're unsure or need time to think, don't be afraid to say, "I'm not sure yet," or "I need to think about it." This honesty prevents you from making commitments or statements that you may not be able to follow through on.

The Impact of Integrity in Communication

Integrity in communication ensures consistency between what we say and what we do. When our words align with our actions, we build a reputation for reliability, dependability, and trustworthiness. People know they can count on us to follow through on our commitments and be honest in our interactions. Integrity in communication goes beyond words; it's about honoring those words through consistent actions. This alignment strengthens relationships by fostering trust and allowing deeper connections to form. It also boosts self-confidence, as speaking authentically and following through on commitments reinforces our alignment with our values. Misunderstandings are reduced when integrity guides our communication, creating clarity and transparency in interactions. Additionally, integrity enhances credibility—when our actions back up our words, others are more likely to respect and listen to us. Living with integrity in communication upholds our commitment to honesty, positively impacting our relationships, self-respect, and the trust others place in us.

Real-Life Scenarios of Saying What You Mean and Meaning What You Say

- **In the Workplace**: Imagine you're asked to take on an extra project, but your current workload is already overwhelming. Instead of agreeing out of fear of disappointing others, communicate honestly. Say, "I'd love to help, but with my current responsibilities, I wouldn't be able to give it the attention it deserves." This honesty shows respect for your time and ensures you're not making commitments you can't keep.

- **In Personal Relationships**: If a friend repeatedly cancels plans and it's affecting your relationship, communicate how you feel directly and respectfully. Say something like, "I value our time together, and it's disappointing when plans fall through." This open communication gives your friend the opportunity to understand your perspective, strengthening the relationship.

- **In Self-Reflection**: If you're pursuing a goal that no longer aligns with your values or interests, acknowledge it honestly. Rather than continuing out of obligation, allow yourself to change direction. Saying what you mean to yourself is just as important as saying it to others, as it ensures that your life aligns with your evolving self.

Embracing the Courage to Speak Authentically

Saying what we mean and meaning what we say requires courage. It's not always easy to be honest, especially in situations where we fear judgment, rejection, or conflict. But by embracing this courage, we create relationships and environments where honesty is valued, respect is mutual, and communication is clear. Authentic communication strengthens our sense of self, helping us move through life with clarity, confidence, and purpose. When we speak with courage and integrity, we're committing to live openly, transparently, and true to who we are.

Living a Life of Authentic Communication

Rule #27 reminds us of the importance of clear, honest, and intentional communication in every aspect of our lives. By saying what we mean and meaning what we say, we're building a life that reflects our true values and beliefs. This commitment to authenticity strengthens our relationships, empowers our self-respect, and enhances our overall sense of fulfillment. Living a life of authentic communication means embracing clarity, facing difficult conversations with honesty, and creating relationships built on trust and respect. When we choose to speak truthfully and honor our words, we're creating a world where our actions, relationships, and personal growth are rooted in genuine self-expression. In the end, Rule #27 is more than just a guideline—it's a path to living with integrity, building connections that matter, and creating a life where our words reflect our heart and soul. By saying what we mean and meaning what we say, we're choosing to live fully, openly, and authentically, bringing our best selves to each conversation and every experience.

Rule #28:
Be kind; treat others how you would like them to treat you (The Golden Rule)

The Power of Kindness

Kindness is a simple yet transformative principle capable of creating a ripple effect of positivity and connection in our lives and the lives of those around us. **Rule #28 "Be Kind; Treat Others How You Would Like Them to Treat You"** is a reminder of the golden rule, a timeless principle that encourages us to lead with empathy, respect, and compassion. By treating others the way we would like to be treated, we foster a world that's more understanding, supportive, and uplifting. This rule explores why kindness matters, how to cultivate a mindset of empathy, and practical ways to incorporate kindness into everyday interactions. When we lead with kindness, we're not only enriching the lives of others; we're also nurturing a sense of purpose and fulfillment in our own lives.

Why Kindness Matters

Kindness has the remarkable power to bridge divides, heal wounds, and foster a sense of belonging. When we treat others with compassion and respect, we create an environment of trust, safety, and mutual appreciation. Kindness is more than an outward gesture; it reflects our inner values and commitment to making the world a better place. Genuine kindness builds meaningful connections, creating a sense of community and mutual respect. It promotes empathy by encouraging us to treat others as we wish to be treated, helping us understand and appreciate different perspectives. Acts of kindness also improve our mental and emotional well-being, filling us with joy, satisfaction, and purpose. Moreover, kindness inspires positive change, creating a ripple effect that encourages others to act with compassion and goodwill. It strengthens relationships by building trust, respect, and open communication with family, friends, and strangers alike. By choosing kindness, we actively contribute to a warmer, more compassionate, and inclusive world.

Cultivating a Mindset of Empathy

To treat others with kindness, cultivating empathy is essential. Empathy allows us to step into another person's shoes and understand their experiences and emotions, helping us see beyond our own perspective. This fosters greater understanding and compassion, enabling us to approach others with kindness, patience, and respect. Practicing active listening is a key way to cultivate empathy, as it involves giving full attention to someone's words without interrupting or preplanning a response, showing that we value their experience. Acknowledging shared humanity reminds us that everyone has their own struggles and joys, creating a foundation for compassion and connection. Reflecting on similar experiences can also bridge the gap when empathy feels challenging, helping us relate to others through our own feelings. Asking genuine questions about someone's life and perspective further deepens understanding and builds connection. Empathy not only enhances our ability to understand others but also helps us respond with kindness, making our interactions more meaningful and supportive.

Practical Ways to Practice Kindness

1. **Offer Genuine Compliments:** Kindness can be as simple as offering a sincere compliment. Telling someone you appreciate their work, admire their creativity, or value their support can brighten their day and strengthen your connection.

2. **Be Patient and Understanding:** Everyone has moments of stress, distraction, or frustration. In these moments, choose patience over judgment. Give others the benefit of the doubt, allowing them space to express themselves without fear of criticism.

3. **Help Without Expecting Anything in Return:** Acts of kindness are most powerful when given freely. Offer help, whether it's assisting a coworker, holding the door for someone, or simply being there for a friend in need, without expecting anything in return.

4. **Show Appreciation and Gratitude:** A simple "thank you" goes a long way in showing kindness. Take a moment to thank people for their efforts, support, or presence in your life. Expressing gratitude creates a positive, supportive atmosphere.

5. **Be Kind to Yourself:** Kindness begins with self-compassion. Treat yourself with the same kindness you would offer a friend. When you're kind to yourself, it's easier to extend that kindness to others as you approach the world from a place of self-acceptance.

The Ripple Effect of Kindness

Kindness has a remarkable ripple effect, where even the smallest acts can inspire others to do the same, creating a chain reaction of positivity and compassion. A smile, a kind word, or a helping hand may seem minor, but it can profoundly impact someone's day—or even their life. By treating others with kindness, we cultivate an atmosphere of goodwill that encourages people to pay it forward. Acts of kindness spread positivity, uplifting those around us and filling them with encouragement to share that energy with others. Kindness fosters compassion by inspiring people to respond with empathy, creating a cycle of care and understanding. It strengthens communities by building bonds and making individuals feel valued, supported, and included. Moreover, kindness inspires purpose, reminding us and others that our actions matter and that we have the power to make a meaningful difference. When we commit to kindness, we're choosing to create a ripple effect that extends far beyond our immediate interactions, contributing to a world filled with respect, support, and unity.

Real-Life Scenarios of Practicing Kindness

- **In the Workplace**: Imagine a coworker is struggling to meet a deadline. Offering to help them, even with a small task, shows kindness and builds team morale. This act of support not only alleviates their stress but also strengthens trust within the team.

- **In Relationships**: If a friend or partner is going through a tough time, practice empathy by listening without judgment and offering your support. Rather than giving advice, simply being there and validating their feelings can provide immense comfort.

- **In Daily Interactions**: Small gestures, like smiling at a stranger, thanking the barista who makes your coffee, or holding the door for someone, are simple ways to brighten someone's day. These acts of kindness may seem small, but they make everyday life a little warmer and more connected.

- **In Self-Reflection**: If you catch yourself being overly critical of your own mistakes, practice kindness by reminding yourself that everyone has flaws and that growth is a process. Show yourself the same compassion you'd offer to someone you love.

Overcoming Obstacles to Kindness

While kindness is simple, it's not always easy. Stress, frustration, and difficult situations can make it challenging to treat others the way we'd like to be treated. In these moments, it's essential to remember that kindness is a choice—one we can make even when circumstances are tough. Taking a moment to pause and breathe before reacting helps reset our mindset, allowing us to respond with kindness rather than frustration. Choosing compassion over judgment reminds us that everyone has their own struggles, encouraging us to see the humanity in others and respond with empathy. Setting healthy boundaries is also crucial; kindness doesn't mean overextending ourselves. Establishing limits ensures we can give genuinely without feeling drained or resentful. Additionally, forgiving ourselves for imperfections is key; we all fall short at times, and mistakes can become opportunities for learning and growth. Practicing kindness, even in challenging situations, reinforces our commitment to living with empathy and respect, creating a positive impact on those around us.

Living a Life Rooted in Kindness

Rule #28 encourages us to make kindness a guiding principle in every aspect of our lives. By treating others the way we want to be treated, we lead with empathy, respect, and compassion, creating trust and positivity in our interactions. This commitment to kindness enriches our relationships, nurtures our sense of purpose, and infuses our lives with meaning. Living a life rooted in kindness means embracing empathy by approaching others with an open heart and understanding their unique experiences and perspectives. It involves acting with integrity by aligning our words and actions with the values of respect and compassion treating others with the same kindness we seek. Each act of kindness contributes to a more compassionate world, fostering a sense of value and support for everyone. Kindness is a daily choice, a path that leads to connection, fulfillment, and joy. By choosing to treat others as we wish to be treated, we create a life that is not only successful but also deeply meaningful. Let Rule #28 inspire you to move through the world with kindness as your compass—a way of being that leads with love, respect, and the belief that small acts can make a big difference. In a world filled with choices, choosing kindness creates a life and a world that radiates compassion, connection, and genuine joy.

Rule #29:
You can't manage what you can't see

The Importance of Clarity and Visibility

In every aspect of life—whether it's work, relationships, health, or personal goals—clarity and visibility are essential for effective management. **Rule #29 "You Can't Manage What You Can't See"** reminds us that without a clear view of our priorities, challenges, and progress, it's nearly impossible to make informed decisions and steer our lives in the right direction. When we bring things into view, we empower ourselves to take control, make purposeful choices, and effectively manage our lives. This rule explores why visibility is crucial, how to identify the areas of your life that need clearer focus, and practical ways to gain insight into the things that matter most. By learning to see things clearly, we gain the confidence to manage them effectively, setting ourselves up for success and fulfillment.

Why Visibility Matters

Visibility is about gaining a full understanding of a situation, allowing us to move beyond assumptions, partial information, or guesswork. Without clarity, we risk making missteps, facing frustration, and missing valuable opportunities. In contrast, when we have a clear view of what we're dealing with, we can make informed decisions, set achievable goals, and address challenges with confidence. Visibility is crucial because it enables informed decision-making, ensuring our choices align with our goals and values. It enhances accountability by keeping us aware of our responsibilities and committed to following through. With clarity, we can work more efficiently, focusing on what truly matters and reducing unnecessary distractions. Visibility also increases resilience, allowing us to anticipate potential challenges and prepare for them, making us more adaptable. Additionally, it fosters growth by helping us understand where we are, set meaningful goals, measure progress, and celebrate achievements. Whether we're managing a project, pursuing personal goals, or nurturing relationships, visibility provides the insight needed to approach life with purpose and direction.

Identifying Blind Spots

Blind spots are areas in our lives where we lack visibility, often because we've avoided addressing them, underestimated their significance, or overlooked them unintentionally. Identifying these blind spots is the first step toward gaining clarity and taking action. By acknowledging what we don't see, we can better understand what needs attention and how to improve our approach. Common blind spots include financial management, where unclear spending habits or undefined financial goals can lead to stress and missed opportunities. Personal health and wellness often go unnoticed until burnout or health issues arise, making regular self-check-ins essential. Relationship dynamics can suffer from unresolved issues or unspoken needs, creating distance or resentment if left unaddressed. In our careers, a lack of clarity about our aspirations or skills can lead to unfulfilling roles or waning motivation. Emotional awareness is another blind spot; avoiding our emotions can create frustration and stress, leaving us disconnected from our needs and reactions. Recognizing these blind spots allows us to address them intentionally, leading to better decisions, stronger relationships, and an overall improved quality of life.

Practical Steps to Increase Visibility

1. **Track and Measure Progress:** For any goal, responsibility, or area of improvement, create a system to track and measure your progress. Whether it's a fitness goal, financial savings, or career objectives, regular tracking gives you visibility over where you are, what's working, and what might need adjustment.

2. **Seek Feedback from Others:** Sometimes, we're too close to a situation to see it clearly. Seeking feedback from friends, family, or colleagues provides fresh perspectives and helps us identify areas for growth we might otherwise overlook. Feedback from others can reveal blind spots and help us gain a fuller picture.

3. **Practice Self-Reflection:** Regular self-reflection is essential for gaining insight into our thoughts, behaviors, and progress. Set aside time each week or month to evaluate your actions, decisions, and goals. Journaling or meditating can help you reflect, increasing self-awareness and allowing you to see yourself more objectively.

4. **Break Down Complex Goals:** Large, vague goals can be difficult to manage if they lack clarity. Break down complex goals into smaller, specific steps to gain visibility over your progress. Each small milestone brings you closer to the bigger picture, making it easier to manage and track.

5. **Establish Regular Check-Ins:** Create a habit of checking in on different areas of your life—finances, relationships, health, and goals—regularly. Weekly, monthly, or quarterly check-ins provide opportunities to assess progress, make adjustments, and ensure that you're staying aligned with your intentions.

The Role of Organization in Visibility

Organization plays a crucial role in improving visibility by providing structure and clarity in our environment, schedule, and resources. When we're organized, we can easily access the information we need, stay on top of tasks, and manage responsibilities effectively. Organization reduces overwhelm, allowing us to focus on what truly matters and make informed decisions. Tools like calendars and planners help us schedule and prioritize tasks, ensuring we stay on track. Budgeting tools offer financial clarity, enabling us to manage spending, save, and plan with confidence. Task lists break responsibilities into manageable steps, providing a clear path forward and reducing procrastination. Decluttering—whether digital or physical—minimizes distractions and enhances focus, creating a workspace that supports productivity. Taking time to organize our lives isn't just about reducing clutter; it's about empowering ourselves with the visibility needed to address priorities and responsibilities with confidence and efficiency.

Real-Life Scenarios of Visibility in Action

- **Financial Health**: Suppose you want to save for a major purchase or financial goal but haven't tracked your spending. By creating a budget and tracking expenses, you gain visibility over your finances, allowing you to manage your money more effectively and work toward your goal with clarity.

- **Personal Health**: If you've been feeling low on energy or stressed but aren't sure why, begin tracking your physical and mental well-being. Note factors like sleep, diet, exercise, and mood. This visibility provides insights into potential patterns or triggers, helping you make adjustments to improve your health.

- **Career Development**: If you're feeling stagnant in your career but unsure of the next steps, start by assessing your skills, strengths, and aspirations. Identify specific goals, such as improving a skill or networking in your field, and track your progress. With clear goals and regular tracking, you gain visibility over your growth and career path.

149

- **Relationships**: If you're struggling with a relationship, whether personal or professional, bring visibility to the dynamics by communicating openly and honestly. Check-in with the other person to discuss needs, expectations, and any unresolved issues. This open dialogue provides clarity and strengthens the relationship.

Overcoming the Challenges of Gaining Visibility

Bringing visibility to different areas of our lives can be challenging. Self-doubt, fear of what we might uncover, or discomfort with confronting areas that need improvement can create obstacles. However, these challenges are often temporary and far outweighed by the benefits of clarity and control. Starting small can make the process more manageable—focusing on one area at a time allows us to gradually build the habit of bringing clarity to our lives. It's important to accept imperfections, understanding that gaining visibility isn't about achieving perfection but about recognizing where we are so we can make informed choices. Seeking support from mentors, friends, or professionals can also be invaluable, as an outside perspective often makes the process less intimidating. Celebrating small wins along the way helps reinforce our progress, acknowledging each step as a success. With patience and consistency, we can overcome the challenges of gaining visibility and empowering ourselves to create a life of clarity and control.

Living a Life of Clarity and Management

Rule #29 reminds us that effective management of our lives begins with seeing them clearly. By prioritizing visibility, we choose to live with intention, taking control of our actions, decisions, and personal growth. This commitment to clarity not only enhances our ability to manage our lives but also deepens our sense of purpose and self-awareness. Living a life of clarity involves regular reflection, allowing us to stay aligned with our goals, progress, and needs. It requires setting clear, measurable goals that bring structure and focus to our efforts. Embracing continuous improvement is also key, using visibility as a tool to refine and adjust our approach to manage each area of life better. Ultimately, Rule #29 is about empowerment. When we see clearly, we gain the ability to make informed choices, face challenges with resilience, and shape our lives in alignment with our true desires. By committing to visibility, we move closer to a life of purpose, fulfillment, and authentic self-management.

Rule #30:
Progress over perfection

The Power of Progress

In a world that often celebrates perfection, **Rule #30 "Progress Over Perfection"** invites us to embrace a mindset of growth and forward movement, rather than chasing an unattainable ideal. Perfection can be a powerful motivator, but it can also become a trap that stalls progress, fuels self-doubt, and discourages us from taking meaningful action. By focusing on progress, we shift our attention from flawless outcomes to incremental growth, building resilience, confidence, and a sense of accomplishment along the way. This rule explores why progress matters more than perfection, how to overcome the fear of imperfection, and practical strategies for fostering a mindset of continuous improvement. Embracing progress over perfection empowers us to pursue our goals with grace, patience, and a commitment to personal growth.

Why Progress Matters More Than Perfection

Perfection is often an illusion, suggesting a state of flawlessness that is rarely achievable. Pursuing perfection can leave us paralyzed by fear of mistakes or failure, stalling our progress and diminishing our confidence. In contrast, focusing on progress allows us to celebrate small wins, learn from setbacks, and maintain momentum. Progress is tangible, attainable, and empowering—it fosters a mindset that keeps us engaged, resilient, and motivated. Valuing progress builds confidence as each step forward reinforces our belief in our abilities and potential. It reduces stress and self-criticism by freeing us from the unrealistic pressure to be perfect, fostering greater self-compassion and inner peace. Progress also encourages adaptability, enabling us to learn, adjust, and improve with each step, building resilience in the face of challenges. It inspires continuous growth by promoting a mindset that values evolution over a fixed endpoint, encouraging us to strive for improvement over time. Moreover, celebrating small milestones creates a sense of achievement, making the journey more enjoyable and rewarding. By focusing on progress, we choose a dynamic and empowering approach to life, filled with opportunities for growth rather than constrained by the unattainable limits of perfection.

Letting Go of Perfectionism

Perfectionism can be a significant barrier to progress, often leading to delayed action, overthinking, or even abandoning goals due to fear of failure. While perfectionism may stem from a desire for control, approval, or self-worth, it can quickly become counterproductive. Letting go of perfectionism frees us to take risks, embrace mistakes, and learn from every experience. Viewing imperfections as learning opportunities allows us to see mistakes not as failures but as valuable lessons for growth and improvement. Setting realistic expectations helps us shift away from unattainable standards and focus on achievable goals that prioritize growth over flawlessness. Focusing on the journey rather than fixating solely on the outcome encourages us to find joy in the process, with each step bringing us closer to our aspirations. Challenging all-or-nothing thinking reminds us that progress is not defined by perfection and that every effort counts, even if it's not flawless. By letting go of perfectionism, we open ourselves to curiosity, resilience, and a willingness to grow, approaching our goals with greater freedom and fulfillment.

Practical Strategies for Focusing on Progress

1. **Set Incremental Goals:** Break down big goals into small, manageable steps. Instead of aiming for a monumental leap, focus on one step at a time. Each small goal achieved represents progress and moves you closer to your larger objective.

2. **Track Your Growth Over Time:** Use a journal, app, or checklist to track your progress. Regularly reviewing your growth helps you see how far you've come and reinforces your commitment to the journey, even when challenges arise.

3. **Celebrate Small Wins:** Take time to celebrate each small milestone. Whether it's finishing a rule of a book you're writing or reaching a fitness goal, acknowledging these achievements boosts motivation and builds momentum.

4. **Reframe Mistakes as Learning Moments:** When things don't go as planned, reframe the experience as a learning opportunity. Ask yourself, "What can I learn from this?" Rather than letting mistakes derail you, use them as stepping stones for improvement.

5. **Practice Self-Compassion:** Progress requires patience and kindness with ourselves. Be gentle in moments of struggle, celebrating effort and growth rather than criticizing shortcomings. Self-compassion is a powerful tool for staying committed to progress without self-judgment.

The Power of a Growth Mindset

Focusing on progress over perfection fosters a growth mindset—the belief that abilities and intelligence can be developed through time, effort, and practice. With a growth mindset, challenges become opportunities for learning, setbacks are viewed as temporary, and effort is recognized as the path to mastery. This mindset encourages resilience, creativity, and a love of learning, all of which are vital for personal development. Cultivating a growth mindset involves seeking feedback and using it as a tool for improvement, adaptation, and broadening perspectives. Embracing challenges as opportunities to grow allows us to tackle them with curiosity and determination, valuing the journey over the destination. Celebrating effort, not just results reminds us that progress is as much about dedication as it is about achievement. Adopting a "yet" mentality reinforces the idea that growth is ongoing, turning setbacks into stepping stones with patience and persistence. A growth mindset shifts our focus from perfection to meaningful progress, empowering us to continue growing and evolving, no matter the obstacles we face.

<u>Real-Life Scenarios of Embracing Progress Over Perfection</u>

- **In the Workplace**: Imagine you're working on a project with a tight deadline. Rather than aiming for perfection, focus on completing each section to the best of your ability, one step at a time. Prioritize progress, knowing that you can refine and improve along the way. This approach reduces stress and allows you to meet the deadline without getting stuck on every detail.

- **In Personal Development**: Suppose you're learning a new language. Instead of waiting to be fluent, celebrate each new phrase, word, and conversation you master. Progress over perfection means valuing each step forward, knowing that every bit of practice brings you closer to your goal.

- **In Health and Fitness**: If you're working on a fitness goal, focus on incremental improvements rather than perfection. Celebrate each workout, each healthy choice, and each improvement in stamina or strength. This approach makes the journey enjoyable and rewarding, building long-term motivation and resilience.

- **In Relationships**: Relationships thrive when we focus on growth, not perfection. Aim to be a better friend, partner, or family member each day, embracing progress in communication, understanding, and connection. Rather than striving for an ideal, celebrate each positive interaction and improvement.

Overcoming the Fear of "Not Being Good Enough"

The fear of "not being good enough" often drives the pursuit of perfection, yet this quest can reinforce feelings of inadequacy since perfection is unattainable. Choosing progress over perfection shifts this mindset, replacing fear with self-acceptance and allowing us to celebrate effort and growth rather than fixating on perceived shortcomings. Recognizing the value of our efforts helps us appreciate the dedication and commitment behind every step forward, regardless of the outcome. Focusing on our personal journey, rather than comparing ourselves to others, keeps us grounded in our unique path and progress. Accepting that growth is non-linear allows us to embrace setbacks as natural and valuable parts of the process, offering lessons and building resilience. Practicing gratitude for our progress shifts attention to how far we've come, fostering a sense of fulfillment and pride in our achievements. By letting go of the need to prove our worth, we free ourselves to pursue goals authentically, with self-compassion and a genuine appreciation for every step of the journey.

Living a Life Focused on Progress

Choosing progress over perfection is a commitment to lifelong growth, resilience, and fulfillment. By focusing on progress, we approach life with curiosity, adaptability, and a love of learning, transforming setbacks into stepping stones and small achievements into celebrations of growth. Living a life centered on progress means embracing continuous learning recognizing that each experience adds value to our journey. It involves celebrating small wins and taking time to appreciate even the smallest steps forward as meaningful milestones. Being gentle with ourselves allows us to grow at our own pace, free from the harsh expectations of perfection. Setting purposeful goals that prioritize personal development over unattainable ideals encourages us to focus on growth rather than flawlessness. Ultimately, Rule #30 is about valuing the journey, honoring our efforts, and finding joy in the process of becoming. By embracing progress, we empower ourselves to face challenges with resilience, pursue our dreams with confidence, and find fulfillment in the beauty of each step forward.

Rule #31:
For true change to happen, someone must wield a sword

The Courage to Create Real Change

Change is often romanticized as a natural evolution, a gradual shift that brings new possibilities and growth. But true change—transformative, lasting change—requires decisive action, clarity, and, at times, sacrifice. **Rule #31 "For True Change to Happen, Someone Must Wield a Sword"** reminds us that change is not a passive process; it demands courage, conviction, and the willingness to make bold choices. The metaphor of wielding a sword is about cutting away what no longer serves us, facing discomfort, and making room for the new. This rule explores the nature of meaningful change, the obstacles we often face, and practical ways to cultivate the strength needed to create it. By embracing this rule, we empower ourselves to make decisions that align with our true desires, bringing us closer to the lives we truly want to lead.

Why True Change Requires Bold Action

True change is rarely comfortable. It requires disrupting familiar patterns, breaking away from routines, and confronting resistance—both from within and from the outside world. Embracing change means taking ownership of our lives, even when it demands making difficult decisions. Wielding the sword symbolizes the courage to cut through excuses, fears, and limitations, clearing the way for growth and transformation. True change requires bold action because it challenges our comfort zones, pushing us to step into the unknown and release the illusion of safety. It demands accountability, as lasting change can only

157

occur when we take full responsibility for our decisions and actions. Often, it involves letting go—whether of old habits, relationships, or beliefs that no longer serve our goals or values. Taking decisive action builds inner strength, reinforcing our resilience and courage while preparing us to face future challenges with confidence. Wielding the sword is also about setting clear boundaries, protecting our energy, and choosing paths that align with our highest purpose. By embracing bold action, we move beyond mere intention and become active participants in our own transformation, paving the way for meaningful and lasting growth.

Recognizing the Obstacles to Change

Change is often met with resistance, stemming from fear of the unknown, attachment to the past, or the influence of others. Recognizing these obstacles is a crucial first step toward overcoming them, as it allows us to confront our fears and build the resilience needed to move forward. Fear of failure often holds us back, paralyzing us with the worry of making mistakes or falling short of our goals. Similarly, attachment to the familiar can make it difficult to let go of old habits, relationships, or routines, even when we know change is necessary. External expectations, such as the opinions and pressures of others, can discourage us from pursuing the changes we need, especially if those changes disrupt the status quo. Additionally, self-doubt can create an inner conflict, causing us to question our abilities or worthiness and stalling our progress. By identifying and understanding these obstacles, we can confront them with clarity and courage, empowering ourselves to wield the sword and clear a path for meaningful transformation.

Practical Strategies for Creating Bold Change

1. **Identify What Needs to Go:** Reflect on areas of your life that feel stagnant or unfulfilling. What habits, relationships, or beliefs are holding you back? Identifying what needs to change allows you to make intentional decisions about what to release.

2. **Set Clear Intentions:** True change begins with clarity. Define what you want to achieve and why it matters to you. Setting clear intentions provides a strong foundation for taking action, even when challenges arise.

3. **Start with Small, Decisive Steps:** While some changes require big leaps, others can begin with small, intentional steps. Each small action builds momentum, reinforcing your commitment to change and gradually increasing your confidence.

4. **Create Boundaries that Support Change:** Protect your time, energy, and goals by setting boundaries. Whether it's limiting distractions, saying no to certain commitments, or stepping back from unsupportive relationships, boundaries help create the conditions for change to thrive.

5. **Embrace the Discomfort of Growth:** Change often brings discomfort, as it pushes us beyond our comfort zones. Rather than avoiding discomfort, embrace it as a sign of growth, knowing that each challenge strengthens your resilience and commitment to change.

The Role of Courage in Transformation

Creating true change requires courage—the willingness to make tough choices, embrace the unknown, and stand firm against resistance. Wielding the sword of change means confronting fears with determination and trusting that the discomfort of transformation will lead to growth and fulfillment. Courage bridges the gap between intention and action, empowering us to take control of our lives and pursue our goals with conviction. To cultivate courage, focus on your "why." Remind yourself of the deeper purpose behind your desire for change, as this connection fuels your strength to overcome obstacles. Visualize success by picturing yourself on the other side of change, reinforcing confidence in what's possible. Accept the possibility of failure, understanding that courage is not about eliminating fear but acting in spite of it. Every setback is an opportunity to learn and grow. Seek support from allies who believe in your goals and encourage your growth, as a strong network can provide the reinforcement needed to stay committed. By acting with courage, we solidify our commitment to ourselves, building a foundation of inner strength that empowers us to make bold, transformative decisions and create a life aligned with our highest potential.

The Importance of Letting Go

To create true change, we must often let go of what no longer serves us. This process involves releasing old habits, toxic relationships, or limiting beliefs that hinder our growth and hold us back. Letting go is a vital part of wielding the sword, as it frees us from attachments that stifle our potential and opens space for new opportunities and growth. The journey of letting go begins by acknowledging what's holding you back. Identify the habits, relationships, or beliefs that limit your progress, as awareness is the first step toward release. Forgiveness also plays a crucial role— whether it's forgiving yourself for past mistakes or forgiving others for their impact on your journey. This act of forgiveness creates emotional freedom, enabling you to move forward without resentment or regret. Embracing a mindset of abundance can shift the perspective from loss to gain. Letting go is not just about what you release but also about the space you create for new opportunities, experiences, and relationships aligned with your goals and values. Finally, commit to forming new habits that support your growth. Each positive change reinforces your decision to move forward, making it easier to leave the past behind. Letting go can be challenging, but it's an essential step in transformation. By releasing what no longer serves us, we create room for true, lasting change and invite a future filled with potential, growth, and fulfillment.

Real-Life Scenarios of Wielding the Sword

- **Career Transformation**: Imagine you're in a job that no longer aligns with your values or aspirations. Wielding the sword in this scenario might mean making the bold choice to pursue a new career, even if it involves uncertainty or financial risk. By letting go of the familiar, you open yourself to growth and fulfillment.

- **Health and Wellness**: Suppose you want to improve your health, but old habits are holding you back. Wielding the sword could mean committing to a fitness routine, cutting out unhealthy foods, or prioritizing sleep. These changes require discipline and sacrifice, but they also create a foundation for long-term wellness.

- **Personal Growth and Relationships**: If a relationship is toxic or no longer serves your growth, wielding the sword may mean setting boundaries or even ending the relationship. This decision can be difficult, but by prioritizing your well-being, you're creating space for healthier, more supportive connections.

- **Mental Health and Emotional Well-being**: If you're holding onto limiting beliefs or unresolved emotions, wielding the sword could involve seeking therapy, practicing mindfulness, or journaling to confront and release these barriers. Facing these inner challenges is a powerful step toward emotional freedom and resilience.

Living a Life of Purposeful Change

Embracing Rule #31 means committing to a life of purposeful change, where we take bold, intentional steps toward growth and fulfillment. By wielding the sword, we move beyond merely reacting to circumstances—we actively shape our lives, cut through limitations, and create space for our true selves to thrive. This commitment to

161

change fosters resilience, clarity, and a profound sense of purpose. Living a life of purposeful change involves taking ownership of your journey and recognizing that you have the power to create the life you desire. It means embracing challenges as opportunities, seeing each obstacle as a chance to grow, refine your vision, and strengthen your commitment to transformation. Purposeful change also requires aligning your actions with your highest values and desires, allowing every decision to bring you closer to the life you envision. Part of this process is releasing what no longer serves you, trusting that each act of letting go creates space for growth and new opportunities. In the end, Rule #31 is about embracing the strength within us to drive meaningful, lasting change. By wielding the sword, we choose to live boldly, authentically, and with purpose. True change may demand courage and sacrifice, but it's through these acts of strength that we carve a path toward growth, freedom, and fulfillment.

Rule #32:
Improvise, adapt, overcome

The Strength of Resilience and Flexibility

Life is full of unexpected challenges, detours, and obstacles that often take us by surprise. **Rule #32 "Improvise, Adapt, Overcome"** teaches us to approach these moments with resilience, creativity, and an open mind. Rather than resisting change or getting overwhelmed by setbacks, this rule invites us to embrace flexibility and find new ways to navigate challenges. The ability to improvise, adapt, and overcome empowers us to face any situation with confidence and a proactive mindset. This rule explores why flexibility and resilience are essential, how to cultivate a mindset of improvisation and adaptability, and practical strategies for overcoming life's inevitable challenges. By learning to improvise, adapt, and overcome, we're not just surviving difficult moments—we're thriving and growing stronger with each obstacle.

Why Flexibility and Resilience Matter

Flexibility and resilience form the foundation of a strong, adaptable mindset. When we learn to flow with life's changes rather than resist them, we become better equipped to handle stress, uncertainty, and adversity. The mindset of "improvise, adapt, overcome" transforms challenges into opportunities for growth, enabling us to remain grounded and proactive in any situation. This approach matters because it reduces stress and anxiety, helping us stay calm and focused in the face of unexpected changes. Flexibility increases problem-solving skills, allowing us to explore creative solutions when things don't go as planned. Each challenge we overcome fosters confidence, empowering us to approach future obstacles with greater self-belief. Adapting to change also promotes personal growth, encouraging us to learn, evolve, and become stronger over time. Additionally, building resilience through improvisation and adaptability strengthens our ability to bounce back from setbacks. By embracing the mindset of flexibility and resilience, we equip ourselves to handle life's uncertainties with confidence and clarity, turning challenges into stepping stones for success.

Embracing the Art of Improvisation

Improvisation is the ability to adapt quickly, think creatively, and find solutions without a predetermined plan. It involves trusting yourself to make the most of the resources and options available at the moment. Embracing improvisation doesn't mean abandoning preparation; rather, it's about staying open and resourceful when things don't go as expected, allowing you to navigate uncertainty with confidence and agility. To embrace improvisation, start by thinking creatively. Instead of clinging to fixed ideas, view challenges as opportunities to explore new approaches and solutions. Stay present by focusing on the here and now rather than worrying about the future or dwelling on the past—this clarity allows you to respond effectively to each moment. Trust your instincts, relying on your knowledge and resourcefulness to guide you through unexpected situations. Reframe challenges as opportunities by seeing setbacks not as problems but as chances to learn, innovate, and try different approaches. Improvisation is a skill that strengthens with practice. The more you experiment and embrace uncertainty, the more comfortable you become with adapting and discovering new paths forward. It transforms unpredictability into a space for innovation and growth.

Cultivating Adaptability in the Face of Change

Adaptability is the ability to adjust your approach, mindset, or actions in response to changing circumstances. It allows us to remain open to new information, pivot when necessary, and embrace change as a natural part of life. Cultivating adaptability helps us stay flexible, proactive, and positive, even in the face of the unexpected, turning challenges into opportunities for growth and innovation. To cultivate adaptability, start by keeping an open mind. Explore new ideas, perspectives, and approaches without being restricted by past habits or expectations. Stay curious, as curiosity fuels a willingness to see change as an opportunity to learn rather than a disruption. Practice emotional agility by acknowledging and processing your emotions without letting them dictate your actions—this helps you manage stress and frustration effectively. Reflect on your experiences, analyzing what worked and what didn't, and use these insights to adjust your approach for future challenges. By embracing adaptability, we learn to flow with life's changes rather than resist them, navigating challenges with ease and flexibility. This mindset allows us to face uncertainty with confidence, turning each new situation into an opportunity to grow and thrive.

Overcoming Obstacles with Determination and Persistence

Overcoming obstacles demands resilience, determination, and perseverance—a dynamic trio that empowers us to confront challenges with courage and clarity. Resilience is the ability to recover quickly from setbacks, finding the strength to rise again even when circumstances feel overwhelming. Determination fuels our resolve, keeping us focused on our goals and motivated to push through adversity. Perseverance is the steady, unwavering commitment to keep moving forward, no matter how slow or difficult the journey might feel. Together, these qualities form the foundation for overcoming obstacles and achieving growth. Facing challenges head-on requires acknowledging the difficulty without letting it define or defeat us. It means adopting a proactive mindset, where each obstacle is seen not as an insurmountable barrier but as an opportunity to learn, adapt, and grow. Maintaining a positive outlook doesn't mean ignoring the struggle; instead, it's about finding hope and strength within ourselves to see the possibilities beyond the immediate challenge. Overcoming obstacles is more than just a momentary act of courage—it's a transformative journey of self-discovery and personal growth. Every challenge we face tests our resilience, builds our confidence, and expands our capabilities. Each setback teaches us patience and problem-solving, reinforcing the idea that struggles are not failures but stepping stones toward success. As we overcome difficulties, we become more adept at handling future uncertainties, equipping ourselves with the mental and emotional tools needed to thrive. By committing to determination and persistence, we shape ourselves into individuals who are not easily deterred by hardship. This journey strengthens not only our ability to navigate challenges but also our belief in our capacity to create a life of purpose and achievement, no matter the obstacles in our path.

<u>Strategies for overcoming obstacles include:</u>

1. **Break Challenges into Small Steps:** Large obstacles can feel overwhelming, but breaking them down into smaller, manageable steps makes it easier to move forward. Focus on completing one step at a time, building momentum and confidence along the way.

2. **Stay Focused on the Solution:** When facing an obstacle, shift your focus from the problem to the solution. By concentrating on what you can do rather than what's going wrong, you're more likely to find effective ways to overcome the challenge.

3. **Stay Positive and Persistent:** Maintaining a positive mindset and persistent attitude is key to overcoming obstacles. Even if progress is slow, each step forward brings you closer to a solution. Remind yourself that setbacks are temporary and that persistence will lead to success.

4. **Seek Support When Needed:** Overcoming obstacles doesn't mean doing it alone. Reach out for support from friends, family, or mentors when you need encouragement, advice, or assistance. Support from others can provide strength and perspective, making it easier to face challenges.

5. **Celebrate Each Victory:** Acknowledge and celebrate every achievement, no matter how small. Each victory reinforces your determination and builds resilience, making it easier to tackle the next obstacle.

The Benefits of a Resilient Mindset

A resilient mindset equips us to approach challenges with strength, optimism, and a belief in our ability to overcome them. By prioritizing resilience, we embrace setbacks as temporary and view challenges as opportunities for growth. Resilience empowers us to stay steady and grounded, no matter how turbulent the journey becomes, enabling us to bounce back stronger from adversity and move forward with confidence. Cultivating resilience offers numerous benefits. It increases our mental strength, allowing us to stay focused and motivated even in the most difficult situations, which strengthens our overall mental fortitude. Resilience also reduces the fear of failure by reframing mistakes as valuable learning opportunities, encouraging us to take risks and explore new possibilities. With a resilient mindset, we enhance our problem-solving skills by focusing on solutions rather than obstacles, enabling us to tackle challenges more effectively. This mindset also improves emotional well-being by helping us process and manage stress, reducing anxiety, and fostering a sense of calm and stability. Moreover, resilience strengthens our relationships by promoting a positive, solution-oriented attitude that builds trust, support, and understanding. By cultivating resilience, we not only prepare ourselves to face life's challenges but also create a strong foundation for personal growth and success. Resilience transforms adversity into an opportunity for learning, shaping us into individuals who can navigate life's uncertainties with grace, determination, and hope.

<u>Real-Life Scenarios of Improvise, Adapt, Overcome</u>

- **Career Challenges**: Imagine a major project at work falls apart due to unforeseen circumstances. Instead of focusing on the setback, you improvise by brainstorming new approaches, adapt by shifting your strategy and overcome by delivering a creative solution. This resilience builds trust with colleagues and demonstrates your ability to handle adversity with confidence.

- **Personal Relationships**: Suppose a relationship experiences conflict due to misunderstandings. Rather than avoiding the issue, you improvise by initiating open communication, adapt by adjusting your approach, and overcome by working together to resolve the conflict. This approach strengthens the relationship and fosters a deeper understanding between both parties.

- **Health and Fitness**: If an injury prevents you from continuing your usual exercise routine, improvising might mean trying a new form of low-impact exercise. Adapting your approach allows you to stay active while recovering, and overcoming the setback reinforces your commitment to health and well-being.

- **Pursuing a Personal Goal**: Suppose you're working on a personal goal, such as learning a new skill, but face unexpected setbacks. By improvising with alternative resources, adapting your practice methods, and staying committed, you overcome the obstacles and achieve your goal, proving to yourself that resilience and flexibility make success possible.

Living a Life of Flexibility and Resilience

Rule #32 inspires us to embrace flexibility, creativity, and resilience as guiding principles in life. By choosing to improvise, adapt, and overcome, we shift from merely reacting to challenges to actively creating solutions and opportunities for growth. This mindset transforms setbacks into stepping stones and empowers us to face life's uncertainties with confidence and optimism. Each experience becomes a chance to build strength, embrace change, and thrive in the face of adversity. Living with flexibility and resilience means recognizing that change is a constant part of life. By welcoming it rather than resisting it, we cultivate the ability to adapt gracefully to new circumstances. It also involves developing creative problem-solving skills, allowing us to think outside the box and find innovative solutions when challenges arise. A positive outlook is essential, helping us approach obstacles with hope and view them as opportunities for learning and self-discovery. Finally, committing to growth ensures that each challenge strengthens our resilience and reinforces our belief in our capacity to navigate life's complexities. Ultimately, Rule #32 encourages us to approach life with an open mind and a courageous spirit. By learning to improvise, adapt, and overcome, we choose a path of personal growth, confidence, and fulfillment. This mindset not only equips us to face challenges but also enables us to thrive, creating a life that is flexible, adventurous, and brimming with possibility.

Rule #33:
Do not thread the needle regarding life events

The Freedom of Living Broadly

Life is filled with significant events, experiences, and opportunities that shape who we are and who we become. **Rule #33 "Do Not Thread the Needle Regarding Life Events"** reminds us not to approach life with extreme caution or narrow focus, trying to achieve perfect control or avoiding risks at every turn. Instead, it encourages us to embrace life fully, taking in all its color, uncertainty, and adventure. Rather than threading the needle, carefully trying to pass through the smallest of openings, this rule invites us to widen our perspective, make bold choices, and live a life that's expansive and authentic. This rule explores the pitfalls of cautious, narrow living, the value of taking risks, and practical strategies for embracing life's unpredictability. By choosing to live broadly, we give ourselves permission to experience life's fullness and variety, leading to deeper joy, personal growth, and fulfillment.

The Danger of Living Narrowly

When we "thread the needle" in life, we confine ourselves to a narrow, overly cautious path, often driven by fear, perfectionism, or the need to control every outcome. This approach, while seemingly safe, can lead to overthinking, indecision, and a life of missed opportunities. Instead of feeling liberated, we become trapped in a mindset that prioritizes avoidance over adventure, robbing ourselves of the fullness life has to offer. A narrow approach to living can stifle growth and creativity, as it discourages us from trying new things, meeting new people, or exploring unfamiliar ideas. This restraint limits our ability to expand and evolve. It can also increase anxiety and stress, as the constant effort to control every outcome is both exhausting and unrealistic. Joy and fulfillment are diminished when we avoid risks, missing out on the excitement and spontaneity that make life meaningful. Over time, threading the needle reinforces a fear of failure, focusing our energy on avoiding mistakes rather than embracing them as valuable learning opportunities. Ultimately, this cautious approach can lead to regret as we look back on the paths we avoided and the adventures we never pursued. Living narrowly restricts our potential and shrinks the richness of our experiences. To truly embrace life, we must move beyond the limits of this mindset, welcoming the growth, joy, and opportunities that come with a bolder, more expansive way of living.

The Value of Embracing Life's Uncertainty

Embracing life's uncertainty means accepting that we cannot predict or control every outcome—and finding peace in that acceptance. Life is full of unknowns, and learning to navigate them with openness and curiosity leads to greater freedom, resilience, and fulfillment. By releasing the need for perfect control, we free ourselves to explore, take risks, and discover new paths. The value of embracing uncertainty lies in its transformative power. It increases resilience, equipping us to handle challenges with strength and adaptability. It enhances creativity by freeing us from the fixation on a single path, allowing us to see and seize new possibilities. This mindset fosters greater flexibility, helping us pivot and adjust without fear or frustration. Letting go of rigid control creates a profound sense of freedom, empowering us to pursue passions and dreams with an open heart. It also brings the joy of discovery, making life an adventure filled with excitement, exploration, and growth. When we accept life's unpredictability, we step into a world of endless possibilities. Rather than being confined by caution, we create a life that's expansive, dynamic, and rich in experiences, embracing the beauty of the unknown.

Practical Strategies for Living Broadly

1. **Take Calculated Risks:** Taking risks doesn't mean acting recklessly; it means making decisions that may stretch us or push us beyond our comfort zones. Whether it's pursuing a new career path, moving to a new city, or starting a new relationship, calculated risks allow us to grow and experience life's fullness.

2. **Set Intentions, Not Expectations:** Instead of rigidly focusing on specific outcomes, set intentions for how you want to approach life. Intentions allow flexibility, while expectations create pressure. For example, set the intention to "embrace learning" rather than expecting "immediate success."

3. **Try Something New Regularly:** Make it a habit to try new things regularly—explore a hobby, attend an event, or meet new people. Broadening your experiences prevents life from becoming monotonous and encourages personal growth.

4. **Reframe Failure as Growth:** Shift your mindset from fearing failure to viewing it as a valuable learning opportunity. Every experience, even those that don't go as planned, contributes to your growth and wisdom. Embrace the idea that mistakes are stepping stones, not dead ends.

5. **Allow Room for Spontaneity:** Spontaneity adds excitement and richness to life. Allow yourself to make unplanned decisions occasionally—whether it's taking a spontaneous trip, going on an unplanned outing, or trying a new activity on a whim. These experiences remind us to live in the moment.

Building Trust in Your Own Resilience

One of the main reasons people "thread the needle" in life is a lack of trust in their own resilience. Building self-trust empowers us to face challenges and take bold actions, confident in our ability to handle both successes and setbacks. Resilience serves as the foundation for living expansively, allowing us to embrace opportunities without being paralyzed by fear or uncertainty. To build trust in your resilience, start by reflecting on past successes. Acknowledge the challenges you've overcome, as these experiences reinforce your belief in your ability to navigate future obstacles. Practice self-compassion, which helps you view setbacks without judgment, reducing the fear of failure and bolstering your ability to recover. Focus on small wins, celebrating each achievement as a step forward that strengthens your self-trust. Embrace the process of growth rather than fixating solely on outcomes. By valuing progress over perfection, you cultivate resilience and confidence, knowing that growth is a continuous journey. When we trust in our resilience, we release the need to control every detail. Instead, we approach life with courage, confidence, and a willingness to take risks, opening ourselves to a world of possibilities and fulfillment.

Real-Life Scenarios of Living Broadly

- **Pursuing a Passion Project**: Suppose you have a creative passion, like writing a book or starting a business, but fear holds you back. Living broadly means going for it—writing the first page or launching your idea—without worrying about perfection. This bold step creates momentum, moving you closer to your dreams.

- **Traveling to New Places**: Imagine traveling to a place you've never been, where the culture and environment are entirely new. Instead of overplanning every detail, allow room for exploration and spontaneity. Living broadly during travel opens you to new experiences, cultures, and perspectives.

- **Building Authentic Relationships**: In relationships, living broadly means showing up authentically without hiding behind masks or fear of vulnerability. Rather than threading the needle and trying to be "perfect," embrace the courage to be real, allowing for deeper connections and growth.

- **Career Growth and Transitions**: If you feel unfulfilled in your current career, living broadly might mean exploring a new field, applying for a role outside your comfort zone, or pursuing further education. These bold moves open doors to opportunities that align more closely with your passions and values.

Letting Go of Over-Control and Perfectionism

Living broadly requires releasing the need for over-control and perfectionism, as these tendencies create narrow paths that make us overly cautious and fearful of taking risks. When we let go of perfectionism, we free ourselves to grow, learn, and enjoy the journey without the constant pressure to get everything exactly right. This shift allows us to embrace life's imperfections and discover its richness. To let go of over-control and perfectionism, start by allowing room for flexibility. Recognize that life rarely unfolds as planned, and be open to new paths and ideas. Detours often lead to valuable discoveries, so embrace them with curiosity. Challenge your inner critic with self-compassion. When self-critical thoughts arise, remind yourself that making mistakes is a natural part of growth and that imperfect steps are still progress. Focus on the experience rather than obsessing over perfect results. Each experience, whether successful or challenging, contributes to your journey and adds depth to your life. Celebrate effort over outcome, acknowledging the courage it takes to try something new. By valuing your efforts, you reinforce a growth mindset that keeps you motivated and resilient. Letting go of over-control liberates us to embrace life's natural flow, enabling us to experience its fullness without fear or hesitation. It's in this openness that we find the joy and growth that come from living broadly and authentically.

Living a Life That Embraces Possibility

Rule #33 encourages us to live a life that is open, adventurous, and brimming with possibility. By resisting the urge to "thread the needle" with every decision, we give ourselves the freedom to live boldly, take meaningful risks, and pursue a life that is both authentic and fulfilling. This mindset doesn't just lead to more joy; it fosters deeper growth, wisdom, and self-discovery by expanding our horizons and encouraging us to embrace the unknown. Living a life that embraces possibility means being open to new experiences, approaching each day with curiosity, and welcoming the chance to explore new paths, meet new people, and try new things. It also involves taking ownership of your choices, ensuring that your decisions reflect your true desires rather than adhering to what feels "safe" or "expected." Trusting that bold choices will lead to fulfillment empowers you to shape a life aligned with your values. Cultivating a growth mindset is key— viewing challenges and setbacks as opportunities to learn and grow strengthens resilience and fosters wisdom. Finally, living with a sense of wonder allows you to appreciate the beauty, variety, and complexity of life, inviting joy and gratitude into even the simplest moments. Rule #33 is an invitation to live fully and freely, embracing the vast array of experiences, opportunities, and adventures that life offers. By letting go of overly cautious, narrow approaches, we open ourselves to life's richness and create a journey that is vibrant, meaningful, and true to who we are. Trust in your resilience, live boldly, and allow yourself to embrace the boundless possibilities waiting for you.

Rule #34:
Ohana

<u>The Power of Family and Belonging</u>

Family isn't always about blood—it's about those people in our lives who offer us unconditional love, support, and a sense of belonging. **Rule #34 "Ohana"** means family and family never gets left behind or forgotten ... is rooted in the Hawaiian concept of "ohana," which emphasizes the bonds that tie us together, reminding us that true family stands by each other through thick and thin. Whether the family is formed by birth, choice, or life's serendipitous connections, this rule speaks to the importance of loyalty, unity, and the commitment to never abandon those we care about. This rule explores the meaning of ohana, the role of family in our lives, and practical ways to nurture and honor these invaluable connections. Embracing this principle allows us to cultivate deep, lasting bonds with those we call family, strengthening our sense of belonging and connection.

<u>The Meaning of Ohana</u>

"Ohana" is a Hawaiian term that embodies a profound and inclusive concept of family. It goes beyond traditional definitions, embracing not only those related by blood but also those connected through love, friendship, and shared experiences. At its heart, ohana represents unity, loyalty, and shared responsibility, creating a supportive community where everyone looks out for one another and no one is left behind. The essence of ohana lies in unconditional support, where people stand by each other through all circumstances, offering love and encouragement without expecting anything in return. It emphasizes shared responsibility, fostering a sense of unity and accountability as each member contributes to the well-being of the whole. Ohana also celebrates belonging and inclusion, ensuring that everyone feels accepted, valued, and embraced. It builds resilience and strength by nurturing bonds that provide support and solace during both joyous and challenging times. Above all, ohana is a commitment to loyalty, a promise to remain connected and steadfast, even when life takes individuals on different paths. The spirit of ohana reminds us that family transcends biological ties. It's about choosing to love and support the people who uplift us and make us feel like we truly belong. Ohana is a call to honor these connections and cherish the communities that shape our lives with care and unconditional unity.

The Importance of Family in Our Lives

Family, whether defined by birth or choice, is the cornerstone of support, guidance, and love in our lives. The bonds we share with family provide strength and security, offering a steady foundation as we navigate life's challenges and triumphs. Within these relationships, we find acceptance, a celebration of our individuality, and unwavering support through every phase of life. Family is essential because it shapes our identity, helping us develop values, beliefs, and a sense of purpose. It provides emotional support during tough times, offering comfort, understanding, and encouragement when we need it most. Families are also spaces of learning, where we gain essential life lessons, wisdom, and resilience that guide us in personal growth. They give us a sense of belonging, a place where we feel valued, understood, and at home. Moreover, family strengthens our resilience, offering stability and courage to face adversity. At its heart, family reminds us that we are part of something larger than ourselves—a network of love, loyalty, and connection that sustains and uplifts us throughout life. These bonds enrich our lives, grounding us in a sense of belonging and providing the strength to move forward with confidence and purpose.

Nurturing and Honoring Family Bonds

The principle of *ohana* encourages us to actively nurture and honor our family relationships, recognizing that strong bonds require care, attention, and intentionality. Family connections thrive when we invest time and energy into them, creating a foundation of love and trust capable of withstanding any challenge. By prioritizing these relationships, we foster a sense of unity and resilience that enriches our lives and those of our loved ones. To nurture and honor family bonds, it's important to make time for each other. Whether through shared meals, regular check-ins, or family gatherings, consistent quality time fosters closeness and deepens connections. Open and honest communication is equally vital, as it builds trust and understanding. Creating a safe space for conversations about joys and challenges ensures that every family member feels heard and valued. Offering support without judgment is another cornerstone of strong family relationships. By being there for one another unconditionally, we create an environment of acceptance and belonging. Celebrating each other's milestones, whether big or small, reinforces shared joy and strengthens the sense of community within the family. Lastly, approaching conflicts with compassion and understanding allows us to resolve disagreements in ways that heal and strengthen rather than divide. When we commit to nurturing our family relationships, we embody the spirit of *ohana*, creating a network of love, loyalty, and mutual support that sustains us through life's challenges and joys.

Expanding the Definition of Family

The concept of *ohana* teaches us that family extends far beyond blood ties. It encompasses close friends, mentors, colleagues, neighbors, and anyone who offers love, support, and a sense of community. By broadening our definition of family, we invite deeper connections and foster a more inclusive sense of belonging that enriches our lives. Embracing friendships as a family is a meaningful way to expand this concept. Close friends who celebrate your successes, stand by you in difficult times, and share in your joys can be as much a part of your family as those related by blood. Similarly, chosen family—those you intentionally surround yourself with—deserve love, respect, and gratitude, as they often become the people who truly know and support you. Building community connections is another way to cultivate a broader sense of family. Bonds with neighbors, colleagues, or fellow volunteers create a shared purpose and strengthen your support network.

Additionally, welcoming new members into your life with open arms allows relationships to grow and evolve into meaningful family-like connections, adding diversity and richness to your *ohana*. Family isn't limited to the people we're born with; it's also those we build connections with. By nurturing these relationships, we create a community of love, loyalty, and mutual support that sustains and uplifts us throughout life.

<u>Ways to practice loyalty and support include:</u>

1. **Be There in Times of Need:** Show up for family members during difficult times. Whether it's offering a helping hand, emotional support, or simply a listening ear, being there for each other strengthens your bond.

2. **Keep Promises and Honor Commitments:** Build trust by following through on commitments. Show family members that they can rely on you, reinforcing the sense of security and loyalty within your relationship.

3. **Celebrate Each Other's Successes:** Show loyalty by being genuinely happy for each other's achievements. Celebrating each other's successes strengthens bonds and reinforces mutual respect.

4. **Stay Connected, Even When Apart:** Life can sometimes separate family members by distance or circumstances. Stay connected through regular calls, messages, or visits, letting each other know that the bond remains strong.

5. **Be Forgiving:** Family relationships are not perfect. Practice forgiveness when conflicts arise, allowing space for healing and renewal. Forgiveness is a key element of loyalty, as it reinforces the commitment to stay connected and move forward together.

Practicing Loyalty and Support

At the heart of *ohana* lies a steadfast commitment to never leave family behind. This principle embodies loyalty and support, which are the cornerstone of strong family bonds. Loyalty is more than just standing by someone during the good times; it means being a reliable presence through life's highs and lows, offering encouragement, assistance, and understanding when it's needed most. Support, in its truest form, requires showing up not only with words but with actions that demonstrate care, compassion, and a willingness to help shoulder burdens. Practicing loyalty fosters a sense of trust, ensuring that family members feel secure knowing they can depend on each other, no matter the circumstances. This dependability nurtures resilience within the family unit, helping everyone face challenges with a united front. Support extends this commitment by offering tangible aid—whether it's lending a listening ear during tough conversations, providing help in moments of crisis, or celebrating accomplishments together. Loyalty and support also reinforce the sense of safety and belonging that defines a strong family. These acts of care remind family members that they are valued and loved, creating an environment where everyone feels seen and appreciated. By practicing these principles consistently, families build an unshakable foundation of trust, ensuring that no one is left behind or feels forgotten. Ultimately, loyalty and support are the threads that weave the fabric of *ohana*, transforming relationships into a lasting source of strength, connection, and unwavering commitment. These qualities ensure that family, whether by birth or choice, remains a safe haven where individuals can grow, thrive, and find solace throughout life's journey.

Real-Life Scenarios of Ohana in Action

- **Supporting a Family Member's Dreams**: Suppose a family member is pursuing a challenging career path or personal goal. Embracing ohana means offering encouragement, believing in their abilities, and being there to support them, regardless of obstacles. This unconditional support reinforces their confidence and trust in the family bond.

- **Being There in Times of Crisis**: Imagine a family member faces a sudden hardship, such as illness or job loss. Practicing ohana means rallying around them—offering practical help, emotional support, or simply presence. This act of loyalty and compassion strengthens the family bond, reminding each member that they are never alone.

- **Forgiving and Moving Forward Together**: In any family, disagreements are natural. Embracing ohana means practicing forgiveness, allowing space for growth and healing without holding grudges. Choosing to let go of past conflicts fosters unity and deepens mutual respect.

- **Creating New Family Traditions**: Suppose you want to strengthen bonds with your chosen family, such as close friends or community members. Practicing ohana means building shared traditions, like annual gatherings or regular dinners, that bring everyone together and reinforce a sense of family.

Living a Life of Loyalty and Connection

Rule #34 invites us to live with a deep commitment to family and to honor the bonds that connect us. Embracing the spirit of *ohana* means choosing to show up for one another, celebrating each other's journeys, and building a foundation rooted in love, loyalty, and respect. Family, however we define it, becomes a source of strength, resilience, and joy—a support network that enriches our lives and gives us a sense of purpose and belonging. Living a life of loyalty and connection involves nurturing relationships by investing time, energy, and love into the people we hold dear. This effort strengthens the foundation of support and creates a sense of belonging that can withstand life's challenges. It also means embracing chosen family— those who, though not related by blood, offer unconditional love and loyalty, enriching our lives with their presence. Practicing forgiveness and patience is equally important, as it allows us to navigate the imperfections of family life with compassion and understanding, reinforcing bonds that grow stronger over time. Finally, living with a spirit of togetherness invites us to cherish the joy, strength, and security that come from belonging to a family, treasuring every connection and shared moment. Rule #34 reminds us that family is both a gift and a responsibility. It calls us to love, support, and ensure that no one is left behind or forgotten. By honoring the spirit of *ohana*, we create a life that is rooted in loyalty, compassion, and an unshakable sense of belonging. Family isn't just who we are born with; it's who we choose to journey with. Let this spirit guide you in nurturing a family bound by love, strengthened by loyalty, and cherished in every way.

Rule #35:
Only Quality People (OQP)

The Importance of Surrounding Yourself with Quality People

The people we surround ourselves with have a profound impact on our lives. They influence our thoughts, attitudes, and even the paths we choose. **Rule #35 "Only Quality People (OQP)"** reminds us to intentionally build relationships with individuals who inspire, uplift, and challenge us to be our best selves. Quality people are those who bring positivity, integrity, and purpose into our lives, supporting us through life's ups and downs while encouraging us to grow. This rule explores the power of quality relationships, how to recognize quality people, and practical ways to cultivate meaningful connections. By choosing to prioritize Only Quality People in our lives, we're setting ourselves up for a future filled with support, positivity, and lasting fulfillment.

The Power of Quality Relationships

Quality relationships are the cornerstone of a fulfilling life, offering emotional support, encouragement, and inspiration. When we surround ourselves with people who uplift us, we are more likely to make thoughtful decisions, strive for meaningful goals, and remain motivated to grow. These relationships serve as a foundation of strength and resilience, helping us navigate challenges and celebrate successes with individuals who genuinely care about us. The power of quality relationships lies in their ability to influence our lives positively. Quality people inspire us to adopt healthier habits, foster personal development, and encourage self-improvement. They provide a safe space for emotional expression, offering understanding and comfort during tough times. These relationships motivate us to pursue our goals, celebrate progress, and embrace personal growth, creating a strong network of support that enhances our resilience. Moreover, surrounding ourselves with driven and motivated individuals inspires us to work toward our dreams and achieve meaningful accomplishments. By choosing to cultivate quality relationships, we build a supportive network that nurtures our well-being, growth, and sense of purpose. These connections empower us to lead a life filled with positivity, resilience, and fulfillment, creating a foundation for long-term happiness and success.

Recognizing Quality People

Identifying quality people means looking beyond superficial characteristics and focusing on values, character, and actions. Quality individuals align with our values, challenge us to grow, and consistently demonstrate respect, kindness, and integrity. By recognizing these traits, we can build meaningful relationships that enrich our lives while avoiding connections that drain our energy or compromise our principles. Quality people exhibit traits such as integrity and honesty, consistently upholding commitments, and treating others with respect. They avoid manipulation and dishonesty, creating a foundation of trust. Empathy and compassion are also hallmarks of quality individuals—they genuinely care about others, listen attentively, and offer support without judgment. Their positive attitude inspires optimism and resilience, helping those around them focus on solutions rather than problems. Quality people also encourage growth, celebrating successes and motivating us to pursue our goals without feeling threatened by our achievements. Additionally, they respect boundaries, understand the importance of personal space, and honor choices without pressure or criticism. By seeking out and fostering relationships with individuals who embody these qualities, we create a network of support, positivity, and growth. These connections enrich our lives, reinforce our goals, and foster a sense of belonging, ensuring that our relationships contribute to our happiness and personal fulfillment. Building quality connections intentionally allows us to thrive in an environment of mutual respect and shared values.

<u>Practical Steps for Building Quality Connections</u>

1. **Be Intentional with Your Time:** Invest your time in relationships that uplift you and align with your values. Prioritize spending time with people who bring positivity, inspiration, and encouragement into your life, allowing these connections to flourish.

2. **Cultivate Authenticity:** Quality relationships are built on authenticity. Be yourself, and seek out people who value honesty and openness. Authenticity strengthens connections and attracts people who appreciate you for who you truly are.

3. **Seek Mutual Growth:** Quality relationships are rooted in mutual growth. Surround yourself with people who are also committed to personal development and who inspire you to grow, learn, and reach new levels of fulfillment together.

4. **Establish Healthy Boundaries:** Quality people respect boundaries, and it's essential to communicate your needs and limits in relationships. Healthy boundaries create trust and ensure that connections remain balanced and supportive.

5. **Let Go of Toxic Connections:** Relationships that drain your energy or undermine your values can hinder your growth. Choose to release toxic connections, making room for quality people who align with your purpose and well-being.

<u>The Impact of Letting Go of Non-Quality People</u>

Letting go of people who don't bring quality into our lives, while difficult, is crucial for personal growth and well-being. Toxic or non-supportive relationships drain our energy, erode self-esteem, and hinder progress. By releasing connections that don't align with our values, we create space for fulfilling and positive relationships that enhance our happiness and growth. Letting go of non-quality people brings clarity and focus, allowing us to prioritize what truly matters and align with our

185

goals and values. It enhances well-being by reducing stress and fostering a more peaceful, supportive environment that benefits our mental and emotional health. Surrounding ourselves with quality people strengthens confidence, as their appreciation and encouragement reinforce our sense of self-worth. It also grants us the freedom to pursue goals, as supportive relationships motivate and empower us to move forward without the weight of negativity. Moreover, quality connections uplift and energize us, fostering a positive atmosphere that inspires enthusiasm and drive. While releasing toxic relationships can be challenging, it's a vital step toward a life rich in positivity, purpose, and genuine support. By choosing to nurture connections that align with our values, we cultivate an environment where we can thrive and achieve our fullest potential.

Real-Life Scenarios of Applying OQP

- **Career Growth and Networking**: Imagine you're in a work environment with colleagues who gossip and discourage ambition. Embracing OQP means seeking connections with coworkers who share your drive, integrity, and commitment to growth. By aligning with quality people, you create a supportive network that encourages your professional development.

- **Friendship Dynamics**: Suppose you have a friend who constantly brings negativity into conversations, draining your energy and outlook. Practicing OQP might involve setting boundaries or choosing to spend more time with friends who bring positivity, encouragement, and empathy into your life.

- **Romantic Relationships**: If you're in a relationship that lacks mutual respect or growth, applying OQP means evaluating whether the relationship aligns with your values and goals. Choosing a quality partner who shares your commitment to growth, integrity, and respect enhances your happiness and personal fulfillment.

186

- **Community and Social Circles**: Suppose you're part of a community group that doesn't align with your values or goals. Embracing OQP could mean seeking out communities that inspire you, align with your purpose, and encourage you to contribute meaningfully, enriching your social circle with quality connections.

<u>Embracing Self-Improvement to Attract Quality People</u>

To attract quality people, it's crucial to embody the qualities you seek in others. Those committed to growth, integrity, and positivity are naturally drawn to individuals who reflect the same values. By prioritizing self-improvement, we align ourselves with like-minded individuals, fostering relationships that are mutually enriching and growth-oriented. Focusing on personal growth demonstrates a dedication to becoming the best version of yourself, which resonates with people who value development and ambition. Practicing self-respect and setting boundaries shows confidence and clarity, drawing in those who appreciate and uphold these traits. Embracing positivity and gratitude creates an inviting atmosphere, making you a magnet for individuals who share an optimistic outlook on life. Living with integrity and authenticity fosters trust and connection, as people are drawn to those who are honest and true to themselves. Additionally, offering support and encouragement in your interactions shows you're the type of friend, partner, or colleague others aspire to have, reinforcing a foundation of respect and care. By committing to self-improvement and embodying these qualities, we naturally attract relationships that inspire, support, and align with our values, creating a network of meaningful connections that enrich our lives.

Living a Life Surrounded by Quality People

Rule #35 encourages us to intentionally cultivate a life filled with quality people—those who inspire, challenge, and support us. By consciously choosing our connections, we build a network rooted in trust, positivity, and mutual growth. Surrounding ourselves with individuals who add genuine value to our lives enhances our happiness, strengthens our ability to achieve our goals, and fosters a deep sense of fulfillment and belonging. Living a life surrounded by quality people means prioritizing meaningful connections that align with your values and aspirations rather than maintaining relationships out of habit or convenience. It involves setting high standards for your relationships, ensuring they are based on shared values, mutual respect, and positive influence. Quality relationships thrive on mutual support, so showing appreciation, encouragement, and care strengthens these bonds and creates a foundation of reciprocity. Surrounding yourself with people committed to lifelong growth fosters an environment that inspires personal and collective progress, motivating everyone involved to evolve continuously. Such a network of quality people not only supports your goals but also brings genuine joy and fulfillment, enriching every aspect of your life. In the end, Rule #35 is a commitment to building a life centered on enriching and empowering relationships. By choosing Only Quality People, we invest in connections that uplift, strengthen, and bring out the best in us, creating a life filled with support, love, and limitless possibilities for growth and happiness.

www.ingramcontent.com/pod-product-compliance
Lightning Source LLC
Chambersburg PA
CBHW062055270326
41931CB00013B/3084